"When I was planting National Community Church, I longed for a resource that provided nuts-and-bolts strategies for reaching people. If you're planting a church or leading a church of any size, this book by Bob Franquiz will help you use every possible means to get your message out and ultimately see more people respond to the gospel."

—**Mark Batterson**, founding and lead pastor of National Community Church, Washington, DC; author of *The Circle Maker*

"The church is filled with theories about how to 'do' church, but few people are writing who have actually done it. Bob has written a book that will help you do what you're called to do as a pastor: reach people for Jesus. *Pull* is practical and insightful and will help you take your church to the next level."

—**Perry Noble**, founding and senior pastor of NewSpring Church, South Carolina; author of *Unleashed*

"As a pastor I am always looking for resources that can help me be more effective in reaching people. I first met Bob Franquiz when he joined my pastors coaching network several years ago. Since then, he has become a trusted friend and colleague. He has hit a home run with *Pull*. This book gives you solid strategies for reaching your community, mobilizing your congregation, and using every avenue available to communicate the gospel."

—**Nelson Searcy**, lead pastor of The Journey; founder of ChurchLeaderInsights.com

"I've been privileged to watch Bob Franquiz pour into God's church, and I'm impressed with the results. He's a pastor whose passion for the church is matched only by his understanding of its needs and how to meet them. God has given Bob an extraordinary heart and mind, and Bob has given us an extraordinary gift with this latest release. Prepare to be challen͏   ͏͏hened, and blessed as you're pulled into Bob's ardent͏   near and dear to the Lord—his cl

—**Bob Coy**, senior pastor

Making Your Church Magnetic

BOB FRANQUIZ

BakerBooks

a division of Baker Publishing Group
Grand Rapids, Michigan

© 2013 by Bob Franquiz

Published by Baker Books
a division of Baker Publishing Group
P.O. Box 6287, Grand Rapids, MI 49516-6287
www.bakerbooks.com

Printed in the United States of America

Library of Congress Cataloging-in-Publication Data is on file at the Library of Congress, Washington, DC.

ISBN 978-0-8010-1560-1

13 14 15 16 17 18 19   7 6 5 4 3 2 1

To my brother, Billy,
who led me to Christ
and modeled what a
transformed life looks like

Contents

Contents

Acknowledgments

*B*ooks are rarely a solo effort. One person writes, but many inspire, encourage, and tell you to get back in your office and keep writing.

To my wife, Carey—You are the greatest woman I've ever known. I am honored to be your husband.

To my children, Mia, Xander, and Olivia—You have brought so much joy to my life. You make me want to be a better man. I'm proud of each of you.

To Mark Rodriguez—You've been with me from the beginning. You're more than a friend and fellow laborer in the gospel. You're the younger brother I never had.

To John Solaroli—When Calvary Fellowship was just an idea, you were there. All these years later, you're still here serving faithfully. I'm grateful for your friendship.

To the Calvary Fellowship staff—Serving with you is an honor. Your passion is inspiring, your commitment is contagious, and your heart for God is life giving.

To my pastor, Bob Coy—You taught me to love lost people and how to communicate the gospel. For that I'm forever grateful.

To Chad Allen and the whole team at Baker Books—Working on this project with you has been a joy. Thanks for believing in me and the message of *Pull*.

To the congregation at Calvary Fellowship—Serving as your pastor is the privilege of a lifetime. Your passion for the lost is matched only by your love for Jesus.

Introduction

Santa Claus, Silver Bullets, and Other Myths

I don't know whether any kid has to be told Santa Claus isn't real; kids usually just figure it out. Maybe it's the milk mustache Mom sports or the fact that Dad puts out only cookies he likes. Either way, kids eventually figure out that St. Nick won't be the one visiting on December 24 to drop off gifts.

The same cannot be said of church leaders. We don't believe in Santa Claus, but we do buy into myths. Unfortunately, these myths don't bring us any gifts. Instead, they deliver pain and frustration. Every conference I've attended has spouted variations of one particular myth. As a result, we have thousands of pastors leading their churches thinking this myth is a truth.

What myth am I talking about? It's that the solution to your church's outreach problem can be solved with one of many "silver bullet" methods.

Depending on the speaker, you get a different silver bullet solution to whatever ails you or your church. I don't believe conference speakers are insincere. I simply believe in the adage that when you're a hammer, you see every problem as a nail. To the pastor/teacher, the answer to your church's growth problem is one of doctrinal preaching. The evangelist says the reason your church doesn't grow is your lack of sharing the gospel. The administrator says a lack of systems has your assimilation numbers down.

I truly believe your church's lack of outreach and evangelism effectiveness is not the result of one problem. I wish that myth were true. If it were, this book would be three pages long and I'd be done typing. But alas, the problem is more complex than that.

When I was sixteen, I got my first car, a 1982 Volkswagen Rabbit that ran on diesel and couldn't be driven more than fifteen miles or the "check engine" alarm would sound because the radiator needed fluid. That car didn't have one problem; it had several. I'm not saying your church is a classic VW Rabbit, but I would point out that a church's ecosystem is much more complex than a car, and as leaders we have bought into a line of thinking that says one idea will fix all our woes.

I planted Calvary Fellowship in Miami, Florida, in September 2000 with seven people (including my wife and me). I have learned a lifetime of lessons in the last decade. I have also coached more than four hundred pastors in one of my coaching networks and communicated with more than ten thousand leaders who have invested in my church leadership resources at www.churchninja .com.

Here's my experience: every church's approach to outreach and evangelism is unique. We all share the same gospel message, but we communicate that message in different ways with different results. I won't insult you by saying there's a one-size-fits-all solution for your church. Whenever I've agreed to consult for a church, I have never walked away thinking, "There's one thing that's going to fix everything here." Instead, after careful observation, I've always found several opportunities for improvement and growth.

In the following pages, I will share with you everything I have learned about outreach and evangelism in the local church, most of which has been learned through the proverbial school of hard knocks. Some of this will apply in your situation. Some sections won't fit your style. But in the words of Bruce Lee, "Absorb what is useful; discard what is not; add what is uniquely your own."

This book is divided into three sections because I believe there are only three types of people in your community. I know you believe there's infinite diversity with people, but I contend there are only three groups in your city. The reason most church marketing or outreach doesn't work is that we fail to recognize these three groups and communicate to them accordingly. What are these three groups? They are the internal, the peripheral, and the external.

The Internal

The internal group are those who already sit in your seats on Sunday. They are regular attendees, first-time guests, or casual attendees who make up your congregation. This group needs to hear the gospel. The primary way they hear the gospel is through the pastor's preaching. Chapters 1–4 are devoted to helping your church see exponentially more first-time decisions and significant spiritual steps taken by those who hear your message.

The Peripheral

The peripheral group are those who know someone who attends your church. They could be friends, neighbors, family members, or co-workers. Whatever the connection, a person in their circle calls your church home, meaning the best way to reach the people in the peripheral group is to teach your congregation to share their faith and invite their friends to church, where they can hear the gospel.

Most Christians live in a world of guilt because pastors usually teach the importance of sharing our faith and inviting friends to "come and see" and experience our services. Yet our responsibility as leaders is to teach those entrusted to our care *how* to do these things. Chapters 5–7 explore this and teach step-by-step strategies for training, implementing, and following up with those who make first-time decisions.

The External

The external group are those who have no connection to your church. The smaller your church is, the truer this reality is. It's easy for a church of ten thousand to say they don't do any marketing. Those peripherally connected to them are an enormous group of people in the city. However, to the church planter struggling to launch a church with his core team, the thought of launching large only happens if he has a strategy to reach those who have no connection to his church.

Here is where direct mail, Facebook, Google, placement ads, billboards, and many other means come into play. This is where we invite those in our community to attend one of our services so they can hear the gospel and, by God's grace, respond to the message. Chapters 8–10 tackle the details of promotion that gets 300- to 400-percent better results than what churches do on average.

My goal is to give you tools that will make your outreach explosive. Now is the best time to reach people far from God. Whenever there is turmoil in the world, tension at home, and uncertainty in the workplace, there is a perfect opportunity for the gospel to offer hope, peace, and reconciliation. Jesus said it this way: "Do you not say, 'There are still four months and then comes the harvest'? Behold, I say to you, lift up your eyes and look at the fields, for they are already white for harvest!" (John 4:35).

The best time to reach out is now. The best place to reach out is where you are. The best church to reach out is yours. You're the right person, at the right place, at the right time. All you need are the skills to do it the right way. Let's get started.

1

The "Un-Magnetic" Church

There is now a level zero.

Master Shifu,

in *Kung-Fu Panda*

I don't know whether it gets worse than zero. Harry Nilsson wrote, "One is the loneliest number," but I'm not sure I believe him, because zero is pretty bad. Maybe one is the loneliest number and zero is just the worst number. When I saw the number zero on a report one day, all sorts of things started to run through my mind. I thought about all the athletes who carefully pick their numbers yet don't choose the number zero. For a totally random fact, the NFL hasn't allowed the number zero since 1973.

So what report was I looking over? It was a report of the number of people who had come to know Jesus since we started our church. The year was 2002, and we were eighteen months into our church plant. My wife and I had left a large church where I served as an assistant pastor to plant a church in Miami. If you don't know, Miami is one of the least evangelized cities in America, so we were excited to go to where the gospel was needed the most.

Well, let me back up a bit. Truth be told, I never wanted to go to Miami. I wanted to get out of Miami. I moved to Miami at fourteen when my mom and stepdad got divorced. Instead of going to high school with all my Red Sox–loving friends in Boston, I found myself living in a rough area of Miami where the students begged the teachers to conduct the classes in Spanish because many of them didn't speak any English. I spent the ninth grade in this scholastic purgatory trying to escape from Miami at any cost. It's not that the people were bad. They just reminded me too much of my crazy Cuban family, and I was looking for normal (read into that what you will).

But one night ten years later changed everything for me. I was asked to speak at a church in Miami in the fall of 1999, and everything clicked. The people in the audience connected with all my jokes. When I talked about weird foods my parents made me eat, they all laughed because their eccentric Cuban parents made them eat the same things. I made Spanglish comments, and they all understood. I began to love Miami that night because I had finally connected to the people there.

After the service, the pastor told me that he had been praying for me to come and start a church in Miami. He had told me that before, and I would tell him the same line—"I will go anywhere God wants me to go, but I'm not going to Miami!" Well, that night my heart started to soften, and I grew to love this city forgotten by most church planters and denominational leaders.

Getting back to that report I was holding with the big zero on it: when I read it, my heart broke. In eighteen months of ministry and weekly services, nobody had made a commitment to follow Christ. (Some people had recommitted their lives and some had chosen to be baptized, but no first-time commitments.) It was one of those days when you slouch in your chair and pray the earth will open and swallow you whole. I knew if this report was correct, everything had to change. We weren't reaching the people God sent us to reach, and a major overhaul was in order.

The church should be a magnetic place. Magnets can make things that shouldn't stick stay together. Magnets can take objects that should fall and make them stay suspended in the air. In short, magnets can allow objects to defy gravity. The church should defy logic and explanation. People far from God should look at the church and say, "I don't understand it, but something amazing is happening there, and I want to be part of it."

That's the story of the early church. The first Christians were a magnetic church. They turned the world upside down (see Acts 17:6). How? It's what magnets do. But our church wasn't attracting anyone. I realized how un-magnetic we were and what needed to change.

The Turnaround

Let me fast-forward to the end of the story, and I'll fill in the middle along the way. In the first eighteen months of our church, we didn't reach anyone far from God. In the last eighteen months, more than one thousand people have made first-time decisions, and more than twenty-five hundred have recommitted their lives to Jesus. I'll bet you're thinking, "What happened?" Like with most problems, the solution required us to adjust several dials to put us on track.

What if you're reading this book and you're stuck right now? What should you do? Let me give you seven actions we took that moved us from being un-magnetic to being a magnetic church.

Confront Reality

Author Max Dupree says the first job of a leader is to define reality. The problem with leaders is that we are so optimistic that it is difficult for us to confront a reality that isn't bright. When I was handed that report, I had two options: (1) tell our executive pastor that his numbers were wrong, or (2) deal with the numbers myself. I chose to deal with the numbers. Nothing will happen in your church until you choose to confront reality.

Confronting reality means you also establish a starting place. The person who wants to lose weight steps on the scale and writes down his beginning weight. The person who wants to be debt-free adds up all her debt and writes down that number. As embarrassing or horrifying as those numbers might be, the people brave enough to know where they start from have an infinitely better chance of succeeding—simply because they weren't afraid to confront reality.

Learn New Skills

Often, churches are stuck because the leader doesn't feel the need to learn new skills. That is the height of arrogance. We must learn new skills continually because we live in an ever-changing world. Rick Warren has often said, "The day we stop growing, we're dead in the water." There are myriad places for us to gain new skills, but we must begin with a decision to stop doing what we're doing and get serious about our growth.

Think about these statistics from the American Booksellers Association:

- 80 percent of all Americans did not read a book this year.
- 70 percent of American adults have not been in a bookstore in the last five years.
- 58 percent of Americans never read a book after high school.
- 42 percent of university graduates never read another book.[1]

Another study reports that only 14 percent of people who go into a bookstore leave with a book in their hands. Shockingly, only 10 percent of those people read past the first chapter.[2]

What do these statistics tell us? They tell me that most people aren't concerned with improving themselves. Instead, they're concerned with comfort and ease. People who read spend about two hours reading each week. Yet the average American spends two thousand hours a year watching television. I tell my staff all the time, "I've never had a problem that I couldn't read my way out of." Here's my point: a lack of education and an aversion to learning new skills are primary reasons churches today are stuck.

Get a Coach

Olympic athletes have coaches. Writers have coaches. Business-people have coaches. People wanting to get healthy get coaches. Coaching is simply a modern word for discipleship and mentoring, where a seasoned leader invests in the lives of younger leaders and gives them insight and training they would otherwise have not received. I talk to many leaders who feel coaching is unnecessary. This decision alone will hinder a leader's ability to lead at a higher level. Everyone needs a coach.

An excellent way to get unstuck is through coaching. Coaching can give you perspective you don't currently have. First, you get the perspective of another person who is not emotionally attached to your situation and tradition. Second, it forces you to get out of your normal routine, and that alone can give you new ideas and insights.

Find a Model

Models are great—not so we can copy them but so we can learn from them. When I meet with a leader a step or two ahead of me, I always ask how he or she worked through the area in which I might be stuck. This allows me to see how someone else navigated the same problem I am up against.

A word of caution here: beware of using theorists as your model. Theorists are wonderful people who give us great insights through their research, but they haven't put their theories into practice. This can be a problem for leaders who read. Although I love much of the material theorists produce about people needing to be in community, when they write books on how to start a dynamic small group ministry based on their research, it is dangerous for local church pastors.

Practitioners, on the other hand, are those in the trenches who lead churches, start ministries, and lead people daily. They come to us with a wealth of practical insight gained from being in the field. What I see lately are more theorists writing from the position of practitioners. One mistake I made early on was reading a book by a theorist and then trying to put his findings into practice. Although his intentions were good, the outcome was disastrous. Why? His views and ideas were simply theories; he had no practical experience. My rule is that if you haven't done it yourself, don't write a book on how to do it.

Check the Gauges

We should be constantly checking particular gauges in our churches to identify problems or celebrate victories. Most leaders simply count noses and nickels (attendance and offering) and try to lead based on that limited data. When I consult for a church or interact with one of my Church Ninja coaching members, my first request of the senior pastor is that he get me information, including attendance compared to the same time frame last year, number of baptisms for the last three years, number of first-time guests per week, first-time decisions by week for the last three years, and many other figures. The purpose is to get a full picture of what's happening in the church and then look at what should be tweaked, overhauled, or blown up so the church can begin to grow again.

Take Radical Action

The solution is not just identifying the problem; it is acting to correct the problem. Too many leaders think talking about the problem fixes the problem. It doesn't. Radical action fixes problems. If your church has been stalled for a year, then a slight tweak probably will not be the solution. It will likely take an overhaul of an entire system of your church to get things on track. The reason this is radical is that people get comfortable, and when you as the leader start to shake things up, it is seen as radical. Radical is good. It's how leaders lead.

When we decided to change things in our church in 2002 and not let the next eighteen months be like the first eighteen months, we changed many things all at once. It's part of a strategy I learned called the "principle of massive action." The premise is this: A typical leader sees a problem and implements one solution to fix it. An extraordinary leader finds twenty solutions and seeks to implement them all.

This all goes back to the idea that the results we get are usually not because of one thing. Instead, many problems must be fixed to get us back on track. That's why the longer a church has been stuck, the more radical the action must be to get the church back on track.

Believe in a Better Future

In his book *Good to Great*, Jim Collins introduces a concept he calls the "Stockdale Paradox," which states that a leader must "confront the brutal facts without losing heart."[3] This is at the heart of being unstuck. You must confront reality, but you cannot allow that harsh truth to discourage you from the future God has for you.

Jeremiah 29:11 states, "'For I know the plans I have for you,' declares the Lord, 'plans to prosper you and not to harm you, plans to give you hope and a future'" (NIV). What makes this passage so amazing is that it is rooted in the middle of a chapter about how the children of Israel were taken into captivity for seventy years. It epitomizes harsh reality followed by a belief in a better future.

The day a leader stops believing that the best days of the church are ahead of it, it's game over. One of the worst periods of my leadership journey was when I was stuck. In truth, part of the story of every church is being stuck. My encouragement to you is not to let it become the overarching story of your church. Instead, let the brightness of the future propel you into becoming everything God wants you to be.

2

Creating a Culture of Evangelism

One of my least favorite memories of pastoring Calvary is our first Christmas service. We had started our church in September, so we were three months into our young church plant when Christmas came. Christmas Eve fell on a Sunday in the year 2000, so we planned our morning service, and I looked forward to a huge opportunity for people to receive Christ.

I had been an assistant pastor at Calvary Chapel of Fort Lauderdale, one of the largest and most evangelistic churches in America. I had watched hundreds come forward when an altar call was given. So naturally I assumed my experience with evangelistic invitations would be the same. Christmas Eve was my first opportunity to preach the gospel and see a large response to the message of Jesus.

As I reached the end of my message, I began my evangelistic invitation. I explained the gospel—man's sinfulness, God's love, Jesus's sacrifice, the need for repentance, and the opportunity to receive God's gift. I called people to pray a sinner's prayer and receive Jesus into their lives. When the moment came, no one responded. Seeing the lack of response, I presumed that I had been unclear in my gospel presentation. I communicated the gospel again and repeated my invitation.

Unfortunately, my encore presentation produced no decisions for Jesus. Then I realized my problem: I needed to be even clearer than my two previous attempts. I delved into a third gospel presentation, and shockingly, no one responded. This was one of my most demoralizing moments in ministry. I didn't understand why no one responded to the gospel. My presentation was clear, accurate, and faithful to the Bible. I had prayed for God's Spirit to move in the hearts of people, yet not a soul responded. It would take me a long time to realize the crux of the problem—our culture.

Culture Shock

If a man takes off his shirt at the beach, no one notices. If that man takes off his shirt in a Cheesecake Factory restaurant, he'll likely be escorted out. What's the difference maker? Culture. The thought of giving children coffee sounds absurd to some, yet Cubans give their kids espresso in their milk starting at age two. Again, the difference is culture.

Culture defines what is acceptable, expected, and appropriate. Culture is a powerful force, and too few leaders give shaping culture the time it deserves. Here's the reality: culture overrides almost everything. It trumps rules, systems, and even common sense.

A few years ago, I spoke with a pastor who was planting a church in Miami. He was coming from the Bible Belt and wanted to launch his church on Christmas Eve. Under normal circumstances, this is a good idea. However, Miami is a unique city with a culture all its own. I explained to him that because of the Latin nature of Miami, starting on Christmas Eve was not a good idea. On Christmas Eve, Hispanics celebrate *Noche Buena*, a traditional family meal centered on roasting a pig, eating rice and beans, and playing dominos for hours on end.

I pleaded with this pastor not to start his church on *Noche Buena*. He told me Miami had many non-Hispanics too. He was right, but everyone—regardless of ethnicity—celebrates *Noche Buena* in Miami. I told him to wait until mid-January to launch his church and then he would see greater success at his kickoff service. He didn't listen to my counsel. Instead, he invested more than one hundred thousand dollars in promotion for his new church. When he launched his church on December 24, ten people attended. Culture wins again.

Sam Chand wrote, "Culture—not vision or strategy—is the most powerful factor in any organization."[4] If that's true, how do you change a culture? How did the culture at Calvary change from that first Christmas Eve service to today, when we see people saved every Sunday?

First, it's important to point out that I don't believe you can change a culture. A new culture emerges that overshadows and ultimately envelops the old culture. In the church world, this is important to understand because we spend needless time trying to change people who do not intend to change.

The culture at Calvary became a culture of evangelism because we focused on new people coming to the church while at the same time teaching our current attendees what the Bible has to say about the Great Commission. What we learned is that some in our church embraced the teaching, and they were excited about our evangelistic focus. Others were indifferent. A few were hostile to the idea. However, as we implemented change, new people experienced only the new culture we built.

Cultural Center

The pulpit is the rudder that drives the church. We shape our culture more from the stage than anywhere else in the church. We create culture through the stories we tell, the people we admire, and the values we uphold. Even more powerful are the repeated actions people see from the pulpit. The most powerful culture-defining activity in our church has been the decision to preach the gospel *weekly*. The consistent preaching of the gospel has done more to mobilize our congregation to invite their unchurched friends than any program could do. When people know their friends will hear the gospel, they will invite with passion.

Here's the question I get regularly when I talk about presenting the gospel weekly: "What if I'm not an evangelist?" The good news is that I'm not an evangelist either. I'm a Bible teacher. I'm most comfortable when I'm teaching Bible background and doctrine. However, the Bible instructs, "But you be watchful in all things, endure afflictions, *do the work of an evangelist,* fulfill your ministry" (2 Tim. 4:5, emphasis added).

Many pastors neglect evangelism because it is not their gift. I assert that even if you aren't a musician, you still make sure there's good music in your church. Even if your primary gift isn't evangelism, you should still figure out how to make sure evangelism happens, which means you must find a way to emphasize evangelism. If you're evangelistically challenged, bring in a speaker gifted in evangelism.

Another strategy is to highlight stories of life change in your messages through testimonies, videos, and illustrations. If your facility allows you to have baptisms during your services, highlight how people received Jesus when you baptize them. The bottom line is that the gospel should be going forth from the pulpit, and we should give people an opportunity to respond.

The Mission

There is great confusion about the church's mission. Many argue that the church exists for the benefit of its members. Others believe the church's mission is primarily for the world's evangelization. I disagree with both positions. Everything—including the church—exists to glorify God. "Everyone who is called by My name, whom I have created for My glory; I have formed him, yes, I have made him" (Isa. 43:7).

The church's principal purpose is to bring glory to God. The expression of that desire is obedience to God and fulfilling the Great Commission. Jesus said, "By this My Father is glorified, that you bear much fruit; so you will be My disciples" (John 15:8). This must be taught from our pulpits if the church is to honor the Lord and reach the world.

When we set out to create a culture at Calvary, we began to talk about the church's mission and purpose. Each year I taught a series of messages on why the church exists. Every chance we could, we talked about our mission as a church. The point is to make sure you present the church's mission regularly. Your church's mission is expressed each week by your actions, by the things you emphasize and in which you invest. If you want evangelism to matter in your church, talk about it, teach on it, and support it in your outreach efforts.

Most pastors do well presenting a mission talk in which they lay out the church's future. I encourage you to remember in your presentation the three things that move people:

1. *Statistics.* Some people like to hear how many unchurched people are in your city and what you're doing about it. This gets them excited and moves them to get involved and support the work of evangelism.

2. *Scripture.* Some in your church, especially new Christians, don't know what the Bible says about evangelism. Teach evangelism, and exhort them to get involved in reaching their friends and family members who are far from God.

3. *Stories.* Stories move us in ways that few other things can. People tend to respond to stories more than to any other means of communication. Talking about life change in a general sense is good. Sharing the story of a person whose life has been changed because of the gospel affects people's hearts. It gives a mission and plans flesh and blood.

Changing *Star Wars*

When someone decides to call your church home, the newcomer takes a mental picture. From that moment, every decision, change, and initiative is compared with the snapshot taken when he or

Creating a Culture of Evangelism

she decided to attend your church. This is important for leaders to understand because when we make changes, either methodically or haphazardly, we alter the picture each person has taken in his or her mind.

Let me explain it this way: I love *Star Wars*. I have every word memorized. I can recite the Bible and *Star Wars* with equal accuracy. Although I know George Lucas is trying to improve the movies by adding a little here and subtracting a little there, it bothers me. I grew up loving *Star Wars* without the enhanced effects and added scenes. I fell in love with *Star Wars* when Han shot first and killed Greedo. The argument could be made that Lucas is making the films better. However, he's messing with my picture.

Lucas's attitude is that it doesn't matter which version you like best. They're his movies, and he will do what he pleases with his movies. This is the exact reason people get upset when we make changes. Our attitude can often be the same as that of George Lucas: we denigrate the past and venerate the future. We say things like, "Everything we did was wrong, so we're starting this really great thing." When we do this, we dishonor those who decided to attend our church based on past ministry.

When we approach change condescendingly, we alienate those who have faithfully attended and supported our current vision. How do you invite people into the future without offending your church's current picture? Simply put, you give them a new picture more attractive than the one they have in their minds.

No one would argue that a child could stay a child forever. Instead, although the child stays the same person, he grows, develops, and changes in ways natural with maturity. Change in the context of church should be presented in that vein. When presenting change, we should say, "In the development of our church and where we are in our church's history, this change is the natural progression for us."

When we launch a second campus, send out pastors to plant churches, or add services, we present this change in the context of a greater picture. In each of these instances, I've said, "One sign of maturity is the ability to reproduce. Although this change might affect us, it's a sign God is at work in us and we're maturing as a congregation." Framing change this way gives people the perspective that although they will experience change, the change is good because it's a natural part of growing up. They weren't wrong in choosing your church, and you aren't intentionally messing with their picture of what church is. This change is like going from sixth grade to seventh grade. Yes, it's a change, but it's a natural and celebrated one. It shows that our past faithfulness is leading us to have more kingdom responsibility.

The Blessing of New Believers

New believers are usually the first and easiest group to embrace a new vision. They are new to the church and growing in their faith, so you can make changes and they will be supportive, especially when the change is to be more evangelistic. People resist embracing an evangelism culture because they believe the teaching will suffer, their family won't grow as much spiritually, and discipleship will be forgotten. Most of your church can be won to this new evangelistic culture through your teaching the church's mission and seeing people come to Christ as you present the gospel.

There is a good news/bad news scenario here. The bad news is that some people in your church will not agree and might become downright hostile. The good news is that they will either leave the church or become part of the minority in a short time. Attrition is also on your side. The typical church sees 10 to 15 percent attrition each year because of people moving, dying, backsliding, or going to another church.

As you begin to reach more people, those people will only know your church's evangelistic culture. I am not saying change doesn't come without pain. We had people leave Calvary because they felt the church was changing too much. You can do nothing about that. Express your care for them and wish them well as they attend another church.

I have learned that people will leave a church for all kinds of reasons. If they're going to leave, let it be because you made a choice that allowed you to reach and disciple more people, not something frivolous. Don't ask people to rip up their picture of church. Instead, ask them to add to it and make it more vivid.

The Most Important Group in Your Church

One group will make or break the evangelistic culture you seek to create in your church. Who is it? Those who serve. Your servants will create the atmosphere that guests experience on Sundays, and they will either heat up the evangelism in your church or pour cold water on the fire. If those who serve don't care about newcomers, they will be cold and indifferent to them when they attend your church for the first time.

However, when a servant believes that what he or she does directly connects to reaching people, something amazing happens. I tell our team all the time that every person who serves on Sunday preaches the gospel. Why do I say this? We all have different gifts and talents, and when those gifts are used in concert, hearts are softened and people respond. If first-time guests arrive at your church and they are treated rudely, it will be nearly impossible for them to hear the message.

If you think I undermine the Holy Spirit's power, I don't. I simply underscore human nature. In the ministry of Jesus, there were many occasions when people were not receptive to his message. In one instance, an entire town did not believe simply because Jesus was headed to Jerusalem after leaving their town (see Luke 9). If speakers aren't wired correctly and feedback develops, the message will be lost in the noise. Distractions hurt the reception of the message, which is why we all preach the gospel wherever we serve. Our job is to create an environment in which the Word of God can be taught—in which the gospel can be preached, in which people can respond to the gospel, and in which discipleship can happen.

As leaders wanting to create or maintain an evangelistic culture, we must do the following for those who serve with us:

1. *Connect their service with the gospel.* I regularly tell our team, "The message begins in the parking lot." That is, we all prepare the hearts of people for the seed of God's Word to be planted. When people see their service as more than a task, they serve with passion. They realize how God has used them in leading others to know Christ.

2. *Connect their service with God's mission.* When we serve, we engage in kingdom work. When we serve those who don't know the Lord and intentionally create an environment in

which the gospel is preached, we do kingdom work. Everyone who serves shapes your culture. You should understand it, and they should embrace it.

3. *Connect their salvation with the service of others.* One of the greatest enemies of creating an evangelistic culture is that we forget what it's like to be a lost person, which is why we should be reminded that the service of others is why we're saved today. Someone served and preached the gospel to you, which is why you're a Christian.

If you came to know Jesus in a church service, there were countless servants behind the scenes creating a distraction-free environment so you could hear the gospel and decide to follow Jesus. The same is true if you were presented the gospel one-on-one. Someone invested in the person who shared the gospel with you. He or she prepared Bible studies, made photocopies, and taught classes that discipled the person who preached the gospel to you. When we serve, our service leads to the salvation of others, just as someone else's service led to our salvation.

Alex led someone to Christ this week and emailed me about it. He talked to a friend over lunch, presented the gospel, and invited him to pray to ask Jesus to forgive him. Alex's friend said yes, prayed to receive Christ, and the kingdom of God got a little bigger on that day.

The email Alex sent moved me. He said, "Pastor Bob, I did exactly what I see you do every week. I presented the gospel exactly as you do at the end of each service. Then I led him in the same prayer you pray each week. I want to thank you for teaching me how to share the gospel by faithfully sharing it each week."

We've come a long way from that first Christmas Eve service. The gospel hasn't changed, but our culture has. Thousands have been added to the kingdom because of it. Thousands are waiting for your culture to change so those in your services can respond to the gospel or have a friend share with them over a meal. The best time to change your culture was ten years ago. The second-best time is now.

3

Preaching That Reaches People

*M*ark and Don are co-workers and friends. Besides working together, they have a standing racquetball appointment every Sunday afternoon at three o'clock. So imagine their surprise when they both attended Calvary Fellowship for the first time one Sunday and saw each other as they came forward during the gospel invitation. They embraced as they prayed to receive the gift of eternal life, and now they have two standing appointments on Sunday. This story again reminds me of the gospel's power and the importance of evangelistic preaching.

Many pastors view evangelism and preaching as distinct disciplines. However, preaching and evangelism work hand in hand. Good preaching sets the stage for effectual evangelism. In the same way, a commitment to pulpit evangelism creates urgency in every message. Famed preacher Charles Spurgeon says in *The Soulwinner*, "I would sooner bring one sinner to Jesus Christ than unravel all the mysteries of the divine Word, for salvation is the one thing we are to live for."[5] Knowing that you will give your hearers an opportunity to receive Christ will influence your preaching preparation and the communication style of your messages.

A girl attended Calvary for the first time in our first year as a church. I'll never forget her because she wore a pink *Sopranos*-style sweat suit and had the New York accent too. She approached me after the service and said, "Pastor, you're a really smart guy." I basked in that compliment, even though I wouldn't admit it at the time.

Unfortunately, she didn't stop there. She continued and said, "Pastor, you're a really smart guy because you spoke over the heads of everyone in this room. I mean, no one in here understood a thing you talked about." The goal of preaching is not to sound smart; it's to be understandable. My goal is to speak so a sixth grader could comprehend everything I say. Some might find this offensive; however, I'd remind you that every major newspaper in American is written at a sixth- to seventh-grade reading level. If people can't understand us, they can't be transformed by the preaching of God's Word and take their next step with God.

Evangelistic Preaching Misconception #1

Some people mistakenly believe that evangelistic preaching is watered down. Nothing could be further from the truth. I teach through the Bible verse by verse and cover topics many churches would rather leave untouched. Evangelistic preaching doesn't shy away from issues that unbelievers won't like. Instead, the key to good evangelistic preaching is to speak in such a way that a nonbeliever understands what's being taught. That means we must define theological terms we use. It means not just referencing a story from the Bible, assuming everyone knows the details. You can't just say, "You all know the story of Jonah." No, they probably don't. Instead, if you mention a story, you should tell the story, otherwise many listeners will have no idea what you're talking about.

The bottom line is that watered-down preaching is not evangelistic preaching. Non-Christians don't want a watered-down message. They simply want to be taught truth in a way they can understand.

Evangelistic Preaching Misconception #2

Another misconception about evangelistic preaching is that it is exclusively for unbelievers. Simply put, believers need to hear the gospel. We never grow beyond the gospel message, not only because the gospel touches every aspect of our lives beyond receiving salvation, but also because we must be reminded of the gospel's simple lifesaving message. One of the healthiest things for new believers is to hear gospel invitations repeatedly in their first few months as Christians. It solidifies the decision they have made and reminds them of the forgiveness and grace associated with the gospel. Regular evangelistic invitations also teach people how to share the gospel with their friends. I do my best to repeat the same phrases each week as well as leading those inviting Christ into their lives in the same prayer; then those who are watching can learn those phrases and use them.

Evangelistic Preaching Misconception #3

Many people believe that evangelistic preaching is primarily based in felt needs. I disagree with that assessment. Felt needs can be an effective tool in our preaching arsenal, but we don't have to preach only felt needs to reach unchurched people.

My conviction is that churches should do evangelism *and* discipleship from the pulpit on Sunday morning. Part of that discipleship is preaching the gospel and inviting non-Christians to come to Christ. The challenge with teaching only felt needs is that we can never deepen the conversation beyond the elementary principles of Christ, which is why many churches have a back door as large as their front door. When people aren't taught anything beyond the basics, they eventually leave the church because they feel as though they aren't growing in their faith, which is why I am such a proponent of expositional teaching through the Bible. It continually challenges believers and exposes nonbelievers to the Bible's truths.

So what does great evangelistic preaching look like? Every pastor who preaches evangelistically is unique in style and presentation. However, if you dig below the surface, they have the same core elements that make them effective.

The Difference between Conscious and Focused

Effective evangelistic preaching is conscious of nonbelievers, not focused exclusively on nonbelievers. This means that as you write a message, you ask yourself, "Will non-Christians connect with this?" You don't ask, "Will they like this?" or "How do I make this palatable for them?" Our role as communicators is to present the Bible's truths faithfully in a way the hearers can understand and respond, which means that even preaching on a topic such as tithing can be evangelistic. Here's what I typically say when I teach on giving:

Some of you here might be thinking, "You're going to talk about money? Boy, did I pick the wrong Sunday to be here." I believe the opposite. You picked the perfect Sunday to be here. First, we won't ask anything of you, so don't worry. There won't be a shakedown at the end of the message. Second, you will hear about the proper relationship Christians should have with money. So if you've watched those TV preachers with big hair and think that's what all Christians think about money, you'll be surprised. Last, you'll hear about why we give. We don't give to earn God's love but in response to God's love. We give because our mission is to reach people far from God and share God's love with them. So you're in for a great experience as we walk through this important, but misunderstood, topic together.

These few sentences not only put non-Christians at ease as they hear a message on a delicate topic such as finance but also give them insight into why this subject is important to tackle. Now they can listen to the message without thinking in the back of their minds that the church will ask for their wallet.

Whenever I teach on giving, I offer this little disclaimer. Then at the end of the message, I challenge these people to give God something much more valuable than their money: their hearts and lives. My point is that your sermon's topic doesn't matter as long as you think through how non-Christians would respond. Then you can prepare them for the message and give them an opportunity to come to Jesus by the end of the message.

Enter the Conversation in Their Minds

Great evangelistic preaching enters the conversation people are already having in their minds. This is where felt-needs preachers do well. They try to scratch where people itch. Effective evangelistic preaching enters the conversation people are having by answering questions and overcoming objections.

So if you're teaching on marriage and explaining the biblical role of a wife, ask yourself, "What would a woman who isn't a Christian think about this?" This opportunity is perfect for dealing with the issue in a way that informs the listener and helps her understand the Christian view of marriage. In your message you may say, "Now, for those of you saying to yourselves, 'This archaic thinking is the very reason I'm not a Christian,' I'm so glad you're here." You've now entered the conversation people are having.

This is so important because now that you've voiced a question, many Christians in your church are dying to know the answer. Their non-Christian friends have asked them the same question, and they didn't have a good answer. By answering the non-Christian's questions, you strengthen the faith of the Christians in your church as well.

A pendulum swings for us as preachers between commentators and communicators. It's what I call the pull between the first century and the twenty-first century. The goal for us is to stay centered so we teach a first-century message in a twenty-first-century way. If we go too far on the commentator side, we just give information with no application and connect people to the text. If we go too far on the communicator side, we give great advice but don't connect people to the text. We've essentially become a Sunday morning therapist. The goal is to communicate the text in a way that connects people to the heart of God, which is important for mature believers, new believers, and nonbelievers alike.

How to Disciple Believers and Nonbelievers

Great evangelistic preaching disciples believers *and* nonbelievers at the same time. We mistakenly think discipleship is only for believers. Think about this: when Jesus gave the Great Commission, he told his audience to disciple the nations. The only problem is that there were no other Christians besides those to whom Jesus spoke.

Discipleship means to teach and train. Believers and nonbelievers must be taught. Believers have many follow-up steps to take once they know Christ. The non-Christian's next step is to come to Jesus for salvation, but often they make that decision after they've been trained in biblical teachings.

Sometimes, when we think there will be many unchurched people at a service, we shy away from teaching and only do straight gospel invitation. Although there's nothing inherently wrong with that, we can miss engaging unchurched people intellectually and giving them some background to our messages. You'd be surprised how fascinated unchurched people are with Bible stories and how they connect historically. As pastors, we unfairly categorize unchurched people and think they all watch reality TV, when many watch biographies and documentaries.

Here's a word of caution: I give a lot of context when I teach, but the information always has to lead somewhere. I never simply teach information for the sake of giving information. Even on big Sundays such as Christmas, Easter, or Mother's Day, although my message is simple and application-based, I still make sure to give context to the passage I teach, and I work through a section of Scripture. It gives the unchurched comfort to know that I'm not playing Bible hopscotch and trying to make the Bible say what I want it to say. Instead, I'm working through a passage, and they can see it. Another important point to note is that if we teach biblical principles when non-Christians are listening, many of them will find that even if they don't believe, those principles work. This helps disciple unbelievers because when they apply what's taught and it works, they see the power of God's Word.

So next time you teach on conflict resolution from Ephesians 4, know that people who don't yet believe in Christ may implement what you teach. They will apply what God says and see it bring peace into a challenging relationship, and that will bring them closer to trusting Jesus for salvation. I'm not saying they can live a godly life apart from the work of God's Spirit. However, I do know that when people who don't know God obey him, it's only a matter of time before they believe.

Aim for Repentance

Great evangelistic preaching aims for repentance in each message. This is the goal of every message we teach. Repentance means to change your mind, and we must all change our minds about false beliefs we've had, false teachings we've held, false ideas we've hung on to, and false securities on which we've depended. The essence of the gospel is embracing Christ and walking away from our idols.

The question I always ask when I prepare is, "What is the false god, false belief, false idea, or false teaching we've held on to, and how does the gospel require us to respond?" When you preach for a decision with unbelievers, the answer is obvious: you want people to come to Christ. When you teach this to believers, it's a bit more difficult, but something always tries to draw us away from the gospel. Our goal is to keep believers and unbelievers face-to-face with the gospel.

Here is one simple way to never let the importance of repentance get lost in the middle of all we teach: make the application we want to give form the points in our messages. I learned this preaching tip from Rick Warren, and it has served me well over the years. When you write the points to your message, instead of making them all begin with the same letter, make the points the application you want to give. Share all the content you want to, but when you make the point the application, you can't forget to apply the text to your hearers. At times, it will even make sense to apply the text before you explain the text. I like to do that because sometimes I give an application, and then I explain the text and its meaning, and then I share another application.

Expect God to Move

Great evangelistic preaching expects conversions. One of the things that has changed since my early days of giving evangelistic messages is that back then I didn't expect people to respond. Guess what? No one responded. Then I realized how unchurched Miami was and how my city hadn't heard the gospel. Even if I wasn't that good, God could still use me.

I started to believe that God could use my evangelistic invitations, and people started to respond. Something powerful happens in a preacher's life when he has confidence in the gospel—not in his ability to communicate but in the gospel's power. Another powerful thing happens in a congregation when the people believe God will move weekly at church. When a congregation believes that the Spirit of God will move and they see people being saved, they will share the gospel with friends with greater boldness and invite everyone they know to church with tremendous enthusiasm.

George was a studio musician who came to Calvary because a friend invited him. He was so far from God that he wrote down a false email address on his follow-up card because, as he puts it, "I was never coming back to this place again." George enjoyed the service, and after a few weeks of attending and talking to loving friends, he gave his life to Jesus at one of our services. His conversion led to his baptism and a hunger for the Word of God.

Fast-forward four years, and George is standing on the stage delivering his first message from the pulpit at Calvary. Not only did he have a message to share, but he also embedded a message. His life is a testament to the gospel's power to change a human life— from an agnostic musician living for himself to a pastor investing in the lives of others. It's proof that strong evangelistic preaching not only produces converts but also produces disciples who in turn disciple others.

> And the things that you have heard from me among many witnesses, commit these to faithful men who will be able to teach others also. (2 Tim. 2:2)

4

Training Your Congregation

I played in a Christian hardcore band called Strongarm when I was in my early twenties. The band gained notoriety and eventually obtained a record deal. Once our first album was released, we set out on a tour all over the United States. Early in our tour, we were scheduled to play a show in Myrtle Beach, South Carolina.

The show's promoters gave us a beach bungalow with a full kitchen, washer, and dryer for the night. The only caveat was we had to clean up after ourselves. In short, no housekeeper was coming to clean our mess.

We decided to walk up the street to the local supermarket and buy some frozen pizzas. After lunch, we put our dishes in the dishwasher and went off to our sound check. Just before we left, I thought I'd be nice and run the dishwasher. Now, before I continue, let me just say that I had never used a dishwasher in my life. I poured in some regular Palmolive dish soap, clicked start, and walked out the door.

When we returned, the entire kitchen floor was covered with six inches of bubbles. As weird as it sounds, God showed me something as I was standing in those bubbles. As a band, we were a group of Christians who wanted to reach out with the gospel's message, which meant we couldn't take the normal "churches and youth groups" route many other bands chose. We wanted to get the gospel out to people who didn't believe yet, which meant going where unchurched people hung out. We played shows with secular bands and performed in bars. In every venue we played, people heard the gospel. It would have been easier to live in a bubble and play only for Christians, but God had not called us to do that.

The challenge my band faced is the same one churches face. We can be caught up in catering to the whims of Christians and neglecting those far from God. Think about when you became a Christian. You gave your life to Jesus, started to attend church, and something happened: you probably started to associate with mainly Christians.

That's what happened to me. I realized that in my zeal to grow in my faith, I had entered the Christian bubble. When we're in the bubble, we seek out a Christian mechanic, hairdresser, music, and even clothing. We think the world is a bad place, so we try to make it better for our family by isolating ourselves from the people who need Jesus most. Many in our churches face this struggle. Our role as leaders is to help our congregations live in this tension of being "in the world but not of it" while fulfilling the Great Commission.

How do we keep our churches motivated to share the gospel? How do we help believers embrace the vision that building relationships with the unchurched is more important than personal comfort? How do we keep our churches from becoming "bubble churches" that unbelievers would never want to attend?

Teach Them to Share Their Story

The apostle Paul was a master evangelist. One tool he frequently used when he shared the gospel was his testimony. His conversion story is told in Acts 9, yet in Acts 22 and Acts 26, Paul shares the story of what happened to him on the road to Damascus.

At Calvary, I use Galatians 1:11–24 as my text, and I also tell Paul's story. There are three simple questions that make sharing a testimony easy to remember:

1. Where were you before you came to know Jesus?
2. How did you come to know Jesus?
3. How has your life changed since you became a believer?

Some people are gifted in apologetics and answering technical questions. Others can walk up to a stranger, share the gospel confrontationally, and see people respond. However, all of us who know Jesus have a story to tell. My goal is to teach our church members to tell their stories and see how others respond.

The great thing about your story is that you don't need a card or notes in your Bible to remember it. It's your story. You lived it, which means you remember every detail and can communicate it with passion. At Calvary, we talk about the different types of evangelism in our new believers' class. Everyone can tell his or her story and influence those who listen.

Give Them Tools

I don't buy into the either/or mentality that says we either teach our congregation to share the gospel or teach them to invite friends to church. We should do both and allow each church member to decide which tool is most suitable for the person he or she speaks to at that moment.

We teach people at Calvary to share their testimonies, and we offer classes on world religions, cults, and apologetics to help them answer objections people have about Christianity. At the same time, we give everyone invitation cards each week and remind them to invite friends and family to church. We also email our church members weekly to inform them about the topic of Sunday's upcoming message.

Teach Them Digital Evangelism

One thing we like to do is leverage technology for the gospel. We do this by using Google, Facebook, and other social media for advertising and to minister to people who are far from God.

Something we do at Calvary is host a "30-Minute Mission Trip." This event happens in our church building, and we invite everyone in attendance to bring a laptop computer. We share with each person the importance of inviting friends to hear the gospel. To make this easy, we even give them some text to use in their invitation. People are free to invite as they deem appropriate, but this helps those who are unsure with what to write. People then use whatever social media platform they have to invite their friends to church. This is far more effective than a blanket email or an event invitation because it's personal.

The evening looks like this:

3 minutes: Change your profile picture to the event photo, which states all the relevant details for someone to attend.

8 minutes: Record a video testimony inviting all your friends to the event. Then tag friends in the video so they will see it.

10 minutes: Post on your friends' walls and/or message them to invite them to the event.

7 minutes: Start conversations with the instant message feature on Facebook. Ask your friends, "What are you doing on Sunday?" and invite them to church.

2 minutes: Call one person and invite him or her to church.

We have found this very effective for us. It mobilizes people to start spiritual conversations with their friends and gives them guidance on how to begin.

Provide Opportunities for Servant Evangelism

Our first priority in servant evangelism is to mobilize the church. People often want to do something to reach out, but they don't know how to do it. Although much has been written about servant evangelism, I want to focus on the benefits of getting your congregation outside the church's four walls. We make it a point to have at least one servant evangelism project monthly at Calvary. This gives people entry points to put feet to their faith and perform strategic acts of kindness in our community.

Often, church leaders weigh the effectiveness of servant evangelism based on how many people attend their church the following Sunday. Although that's not a bad metric, it's certainly not the only measurement worth noting. We have found that those who participate are more likely to serve in the church, get into a small group, and take spiritual growth seriously.

One benefit of living in South Florida is the ability to do outdoor servant evangelism projects regularly. One Saturday a month, for a three-hour period, we occupy a street corner in our community and give away hundreds of bottles of cold water with invitations to our church during a three-hour project.

One Saturday, we gave a bottle of water and an invitation to a local police officer. He attended church the next day and gave his life to Jesus. The following month, he handed out bottles of water with the team. One thing we've seen is that those reached by water distribution are passionate about this servant evangelism project. In fact, the church rarely has to buy the water to distribute. Those who participate usually buy it as an act of service to the Lord.

Some time ago, we organized a prayer walk in our community. Many people attended armed with invitations in case they found someone to ask to church. As one group was passed by a car, they saw the window was cracked open. On a whim, someone from the group dropped a card through the crack. A man named Fernando was sitting in the backseat and the card landed on his lap. What no one knew was that Fernando had prayed for God to lead him to a church where he could grow in his new relationship with Jesus. God literally dropped a Calvary invitation card on his lap while he was praying!

Today, Fernando is a drummer on our worship team, and his entire family attends Calvary and serves in various areas of ministry. Servant evangelism is a win-win for everyone. It's a win for the person receiving the ministry, and it's a win for the person doing the ministry. They are energized and blessed that God uses them.

Model the Lifestyle

We can talk about evangelizing, inviting people to church, and doing service projects all day, but what really grips the hearts of people is when we model an evangelistic lifestyle. I learned this lesson several years ago when I told the story of a man I met at a baseball game. I attended the game with some friends, and we were able to sit in the stadium owner's skybox. We were catered to in every way and got to watch the game from comfy couches.

During the game, I spoke with the owner, and he began to tell me about his business exploits and his hobbies. He loved to go to championship games of all major sporting events. He had attended the World Series, NBA Championship, NHL Finals, and several Super Bowls.

As he told me of his sporting attendance, he said, "Have you ever attended the Kentucky Derby?" I said, "No, but I did work at Kentucky Fried Chicken in high school." The conversation turned to my life and background. When the moment was right, I shared my story of faith. In the context of telling him my background, I was able to present the gospel to him. He was intrigued, and we agreed to talk further about some questions he had about faith and Christianity.

In the weeks that followed my sharing this story at our church, evangelism exploded. People invited friends as never before. Each week, people tracked me down to tell their story of sharing their faith. One simple story opened the floodgates because the senior leader took evangelism seriously. This is the power of modeling an evangelistic lifestyle. Now I regularly tell stories of sharing my faith because they energize our congregation and keep the value of evangelism high in our church.

We are all believers today because someone took the time to share the gospel with us. Whether from a parent or pastor, co-worker or classmate, friend or family member, we all heard the same message of salvation and the same offer of forgiveness and eternal life. Christianity progresses because God's people cannot contain the message of God's grace. By the Holy Spirit's power, they share the right words at the right time, and God uses them to change people's lives all over the world. If you trace your spiritual lineage far enough, you'll end up in Galilee with twelve men listening to Jesus and learning what the kingdom of God is. Our churches are part of that unbroken lineage, and it is by God working through his people that men and women encounter Jesus today.

I met Steve in the ninth grade. He was the first Christian I ever met. He was a nice guy, and he constantly told me of my need for Jesus. He shared with me the story of how he came to know Christ and told me about his church.

One Wednesday evening, Steve asked if I would give him a ride to church. I declined and told him I was busy. Steve then said, "Come on, Bob. I'll give you five bucks if you give me a ride." Those were the magic words because the next thing I said was, "What time would you like me to pick you up?"

We drove to his church (which was forty-five minutes away), and he preached the gospel to me the entire time. A few weeks later, on my sixteenth birthday, he gave me a Bible. On the inside cover he wrote, "Of all 66 books of the Bible, I hope you find only 1 thing: Jesus Christ. Your friend, Steve." This inscription is the only one I've ever committed to memory, and that Bible sits in my office within arm's reach. It reminds me of how one person can meet Jesus and that story can influence the lives of countless others.

5

How to Have More Than One Easter
a Year

I wish every Sunday could be like Easter.

Every pastor who has ever lived

*I*n 2003, I made the mistake of spending New Year's Eve at Disney World. Although I'm a big Disney fan, I'm not very fond of being inside the Magic Kingdom when it feels like the mosh pit at a Metallica concert. The park was at capacity. That means Disney cast members only let people enter the park when someone exited. Every ride had a minimum forty-five-minute wait. I'm sure somewhere the Disney CFO is saying, "I wish every day could be like New Year's Eve."

Likewise, restaurant owners all dream for every night to be like Saturday night. Unfortunately, every night can't be the "big night." However, that doesn't mean every night has to be slow and deserted. Restaurants use strategies to fill their dining rooms on slow nights.

Carey and I enjoy a restaurant down the street from our house. They know Tuesday night is slow, so they started a "kids eat free" promotion on Tuesdays. Although Tuesday night isn't typically a night we go out to eat, if we do go out on a Tuesday, we usually go there. Here's what's funny—the last time we dined out on a Tuesday night, the restaurant was full. It was certainly busier than most other restaurants on a Tuesday. Hotels, theme parks, and every other industry have nonpeak seasons, and they don't have the luxury to wait for the business to come to them. If they don't get customers, they end up shutting down.

Churches have slow seasons just like everyone else. Summer, long weekends, holidays, and teacher planning days can cause our attendance to look like a tachycardic EKG report. Not every Sunday can be exactly like Easter. Easter is a very special day. It's like wishing every football game were like the Super Bowl. If every game were the Super Bowl, then the Super Bowl would cease to be the special game it is.

If we used the strategies we use on Easter, we'd see a bigger turnout during other times of the year. Some Sundays will have low attendance no matter what, and that's okay. Just accept it.

The Sunday after Thanksgiving is the lowest-attended church service of the year in America. Attendance is so low most years that I've renamed that day "National Associate Pastor Preaching Sunday." The Sunday after Thanksgiving has been our week to give the pulpit to a new teacher on our staff. It has also been our time to let a new worship leader lead the band. And it is a great Sunday for senior pastors to rest and prepare for a strong Christmas season.

One of the most important ideas you'll learn in this chapter is that no church grows fifty-two weeks a year. Instead, the life of every church has seasons of sowing, planting, and watering and times of reaping and rewards.

One mistake I see church leaders make is trying to hype every Sunday. Communicating to your church that this Sunday could be the greatest service in your church's history is fine, but you can't say that weekly or people will stop believing you. Once that happens, you become the pastor who cried wolf. When you do have a big event you're promoting, no one will listen because you burned through all your relational equity by hyping every Sunday. In contrast, there are several times a year you can create major momentum by focusing on a special Sunday and creating an Easter-like environment that propels your church to the next level.

Great leaders shine when they take a slump and turn it into a surge. Disney does this masterfully. In 2008, when the economy was headed south and Disney was almost forced to lay off its "cast members" (or employees), it instituted a "get in free on your birthday" promotion. Within days, their parks, hotels, and restaurants were at capacity. Churches can use different strategies and see similar results on Sundays that aren't being used to their fullest potential. Imagine having an "Easter effect" on several Sundays throughout the year, seeing your auditorium filled and reaching people who normally would not be reached.

Understand the Times

On many Sundays throughout the year, you can create Easter-like momentum in your church. Some churches give up entirely on the summer because there are a few weeks when attendance will be lower. I've been in ministry long enough to know that on some Sundays during the summer, your church will be a ghost town. Yet, other summer Sundays can be huge in your church. Many people go on vacation the first two Sundays after school lets out and the two Sundays before school starts in the fall. Apart from those four Sundays and Fourth of July weekend, the rest of the summer can be used for big Sundays and reaching many people in your community. Too often pastors miss this pattern and unwisely take July off for vacation. You are much better off taking parts of August for vacation and staying in town during July so you can plan some momentum-building Sundays into your calendar.

Realize There Will Always Be Fluctuations

Pastors drive themselves crazy judging their attendance week to week. If you do this, I can promise you will be discouraged. Instead, as you get some history in your church, track this week's numbers by this week last year. Look at your giving by what's happening this quarter.

I spoke with a pastor recently who thought his church was going under because giving was down. I asked him how long the pattern had been going. He said, "Three weeks!" You will go nuts living like this. The beauty of tracking things from the beginning is you can see the long-term ebbs and flows of church metrics.

I'm surprised how many churches don't do anything special on the first Sunday in November, the Sunday that ends daylight saving time (and everyone gets an extra hour of sleep). Each year we create a mini-Easter on this weekend, and we have seen tremendous results.

You don't even have to be that elaborate. Just to prove the point, three years ago we did an event called Hot Dog Day. I don't know whether there's a worse name than Hot Dog Day, but we promoted Hot Dog Day on the first Sunday in November, and we had a 20 percent boost in attendance. We took an average Sunday and made it a mini-Easter because we emphasized it and promoted it. The result was a big win for the church and many people reached for the kingdom.

Wise pastors monitor their attendance fluctuations and pick good Sundays to promote as special Sundays. I know one pastor who consistently picks the worst Sundays to start new series or promote events. He will start a new series on Memorial Day weekend, Super Bowl Sunday, and Labor Day weekend. Then he calls me to lament his limited results. My encouragement to him is to let these Sundays be lower Sundays and focus on the Sundays that can be maximized.

Consider the movie industry. There's a reason most big blockbusters are released during the summer. Filmmakers understand that people have more free time during the summer and will watch more movies. They aren't trying to bolster their March releases. Instead, they know some weekends are bad for movies, so they focus on the weekends they can gather a larger audience.

Hold Once-a-Year Events

There's a reason Easter is such a big Sunday: it happens only once a year. If Easter was once a month, it wouldn't have the same effect. When you plan a big event and seek to create a mini-Easter, do something that happens only once a year.

Every Mother's Day, we offer free family portraits for the entire church. After posing for their photo, each family is given a card with a website where they can download their portrait. Sometimes families are out of town and ask when we are taking family portraits again. We respond, "Next Mother's Day." Doing another family portrait event would weaken the Mother's Day outreach we do. We do an Easter egg hunt on Easter, so we're not going to do a Christmas ornament hunt later in the year. The key is to create something special that happens only once a year so people feel as if they're missing out if they don't show up.

Allow me to give you the other side of this: make the service on that special day as normal as possible. The senior pastor should speak. The worship leader should lead the music. The service should be as normal as possible so that guests can see what your church is like on a typical weekend. I know pastors who bring in special speakers on major Sundays and see little net effect afterward. The simple reason is that when guests return after that special event, they hear someone other than the speaker they connected with originally. There are times to bring in speakers and musicians, but try to make your special Sundays as ordinary as possible.

Every Sunday at your church, you should make sure you deliver top-notch quality in your music and preaching. There are Sundays to debut new teachers or musicians, but they must be ready to give their best effort. One reason churches slump over the summer is that people see leaders who are still developing for most of those weeks. Instead, the senior pastor and worship pastor should only miss weeks when most people will be away. You can have newer communicators and musicians lead those weeks.

No matter what, your quality level should be high because every week there's going to be someone who is a first-time guest in your church. Joe DiMaggio was once asked why he gave his best effort each game. He replied, "There is always some kid who may be seeing me for the first time. I owe him my best."[6]

The same principle applies to church leaders. We owe God our best, and when we give our best, he uses it. We must treat every Sunday as important. Many churches don't grow because they simply don't believe that every Sunday matters. You must believe your church service is the most important hour in your community. Nothing else is more important. This will also influence how or what you advertise to your community. We promote only our Sunday services because that's when people hear the gospel. We might have other things going on, but the thrust of all our promotion is always the Sunday service.

Create Your Own Holidays

We are notorious for creating our own holidays at Calvary. Hot Dog Day was one example. Another Sunday we take advantage of is our church anniversary. We make this the second-biggest day of the year after Easter. What would normally be just a regular Sunday in September is now a huge day for us. I have a friend whose church's anniversary is in mid-June, and his church is packed to the gills in the middle of the summer. His church grows because he created his own holiday.

February is another good month. Our February relationship series is something everyone looks forward to. It has now reached holiday status. We kick the series off the Sunday before Valentine's

Day, and it's one of our biggest Sundays of the year. Before we did Christmas Eve services, we celebrated the day before Christmas Eve and called it Christmas Eve-Eve. To this day, Christmas Eve-Eve is still better attended than our Christmas Eve services. When you make a day special, it's contagious.

Understand the Anatomy of a Big Sunday

The key to creating a mini-Easter is to pick the right Sunday, mobilize your congregation, and create a sense of urgency. On a practical level, this is why Easter is such a huge success. People believe their friends are more open to attending church on Easter (which is true), and this greatly motivates them to invite their friends.

Our offer of free family portraits on Mother's Day creates a sense of urgency for entire families to attend church because we give away a free 8 x 10 picture. The fact that mom says, "All I want for Mother's Day is for my whole family to come to church" doesn't hurt either. You can get people to invite friends more on these days than on others. We must create a rhythm of tension and release in our churches. When you're doing a big Sunday, ramp it up and let people know what to expect. Give them all the benefits of what will happen if they attend and if they invite their friends.

Plan for the Event

A minute's worth of planning is worth an hour of execution. Give yourself enough time to make these events successful. You can't pull off a big Sunday in a week. You probably need six weeks to plan a big Sunday properly. What goes into planning an event like this?

1. Put the date on the calendar at least six weeks out.
2. Put together a marketing plan for the event.
3. Plan how you will communicate the event to your church.
4. Create a look for the event (graphics, banners, posters, etc.).
5. Organize any special elements (food, sound system, staging) needed for the event.
6. Buy anything you need to make this event happen.
7. Find extra people to serve.
8. Determine how this service will affect your children's ministry or child care.
9. Create tools for people to invite friends.
10. Think through every aspect of your service from start to finish.

Create a Mini-Easter Calendar

The following is a quick overview of which Sundays are generally great weeks to plan a mini-Easter:

January: The Sunday after Martin Luther King weekend. This Sunday is huge for us at Calvary. While I don't advise bringing in a guest speaker for this big day, we usually bring in a speaker to create some excitement for our big day in February.

February: The Sunday after the Super Bowl is one of our biggest days of the year. We usually kick off a series on relationships. We promote this weekend in a big way because the size of that day affects the size of Easter (which is a few weeks later).

March: We usually teach evangelism in March, so there's a larger than usual service there, allowing us to prepare our congregation for Easter. It allows us to motivate our church to invite everyone they know to hear the gospel on Easter too.

April: Easter is usually in April, so that's the weekend we invest in most during this month. For Easter, we pull out all the stops and promote, invite, and invest in reaching people like no other time of the year.

May: Mother's Day is the day we focus on most in May. It is one of the best Sundays of the year to reach families.

June: In June, we focus on Father's Day. It won't be as powerful as Mother's Day, but Father's Day can still have a big impact. Often, we give away a men's book to every man who attends. That doesn't mean much to the unchurched person in your neighborhood, but it means a lot to your regular attendees who know that book's impact. Some churches have contests and give away prizes from grills to motorcycles. Sometimes these giveaways get the church excited and motivate people to invite their dads to attend.

July: Two weeks after Independence Day weekend is a great weekend to have a big Sunday. July is the month in which you see attendance surge over the summer. Capitalize on that momentum and have a barbecue and baptism Sunday. Attendance might be low at times over the summer, but we baptize more people during the summer months than any other time during the year.

August: School starts in mid-August in Florida, so late August is a great time to kick off a series of teachings. I usually teach on stewardship for three to four weeks around this time of year.

September: Two weeks after Labor Day can be a huge Sunday for your church if you promote it well. You'll see a bump as people get back into the swing of things with school starting. If you intentionally invest in this day, you'll see huge dividends. We usually do a spiritual growth campaign during the fall, so this is a big weekend in our calendar.

October: Except for Columbus Day weekend, any weekend in October is good for doing a big day and having great results. You should be hitting your stride here in the fall season. Often, we bring in a guest speaker to mix things up and create some excitement in the church.

November: As I mentioned earlier, the first Sunday of November marks the end of daylight saving time, and everyone gets an extra hour of sleep. This is one of my favorite Sundays of the year. Do something special on this day, and you'll reach many people. Because of the extra hour of sleep, it's also a great Sunday to reach unchurched people because they won't oversleep.

December: Christmas Eve is the day in which to invest for December. I encourage you to do something that involves kids singing. Even people with the most hardened hearts will come to church to hear their children sing in the service. We have many stories in our church of men who came only to hear their son or daughter sing on Christmas Eve, but when they heard the gospel message, they responded and gave their lives to Jesus.

Rizo gave his life to Jesus two years ago at Calvary. When he heard about our free Mother's Day portraits, he saw it as an opportunity to reach his family. He made it his mission to invite every member of his family. On Mother's Day, one of our pastors asked me to walk to the area on our campus where the portraits were being taken. When I got there, I saw Rizo standing with twenty-two family members. Later he told me, "Pastor Bob, I've been trying to get my family to attend church for a year. This free picture did what my invitations couldn't do alone. Today, every member of my family heard the gospel, and several responded to God's call."

Here's the bottom line: your church should have twelve to fifteen Easters a year. Use the calendar and some creativity to reach more people by making strategic Sundays have an Easter-like impact in your community.

6

No New Believer Left Behind

*A*t Calvary, we've created an eight-step process for those who decide to follow Jesus. Although you can reach thousands of people at one time, if you don't have a follow-up process that works, they will leave out the back door as quickly as they entered.

The greatest stewardship we are given is the stewardship of people. Churches should receive new believers as gifts from God. As church leaders, our goal is to give new believers what they need to take their first steps with Jesus in the world in which we live. It is with that heart that we developed what we call the eight "ates" of new believer follow-up.

1. Indicate

If you miss any of the eight steps, don't miss this one. This one is the most important because without this step, it is nearly impossible to have meaningful follow-up. When people decide to follow Jesus, you must give them an opportunity to indicate that decision somehow.

At Calvary, we encourage people to indicate their decision on our connection card. This card is given to people as they enter the service. A typical connection card has a place for attendees to add their contact information as well as indicate what "next step" they are taking. Even those who come forward when we give our gospel invitations fill out the connection card when we take them to our follow-up area and give them a Bible. This is so vital because once people fill out that card, you now have a way to follow up with them by their method of choice: email, phone call, or letter that's mailed to them.

One question I receive from pastors in my Church Ninja coaching network is, "What if people don't want to fill out the connection card?" My response is, "Give them a reason to fill it out." You won't have very many people filling out the card if the only benefit is for the church. Instead, we regularly say that the connection card is a statement of faith. God is challenging them to take the next step. Our goal is to help them follow his leading.

One of the best motivators for people to fill out the connection card is to offer a free resource that will help them grow in the decision they just made. This can be a book, CD, or DVD, but it should be something they find valuable enough to trust you with their contact information. We also make the card simple to fill out. We don't ask for needless data we won't use.

One challenge with new believer follow-up is that those who decide to follow Jesus can't completely articulate what they just experienced. They know God spoke to them, and they were moved during the service, but they don't have the words to explain it. This is where a strong follow-up process comes into play and helps new believers understand what they've experienced.

Remember the parable of the sower:

> This is the meaning of the parable: The seed is the word of God. Those along the path are the ones who hear, and then the devil comes and takes away the word from their hearts, so that they may not believe and be saved. Those on the rocky ground are the ones who receive the word with joy when they hear it, but they have no root. They believe for a while, but in the time of testing they fall away. (Luke 8:11–13 NIV)

We can't do anything about those who don't receive the Word, but those who do receive it need follow-up. Our goal should be to create a process through which new believers can dig roots and grow in their faith.

2. Congratulate

Once people indicate their decision to follow Jesus, our goal is to contact and congratulate them within twenty-four hours. When people walk to the front in our services at Calvary, everyone claps, shouts, and rejoices. I tell those who have responded to the invitation that the reason people are excited over their decision is that the Bible says there's a party happening in heaven right now. "In the same way, I tell you, there is rejoicing in the presence of the angels of God over one sinner who repents" (Luke 15:10 NIV).

Salvation is something celebrated in heaven, and we should do the same. When we contact those who made a decision over the weekend, it reminds them of the decision they made and the experience they had during the service. If we lead people to Christ and fail to connect them to a local church, we have done them a disservice. Without participation in a local church, new believers do not grow to maturity.

When we contact someone who just made a decision, we want to do five things:

1. Congratulate them on the decision they made on Sunday. I typically share a Scripture, such as 2 Corinthians 5:17: "Therefore, if anyone is in Christ, the new creation has come: The old has gone, the new is here!" (NIV).

2. Remind them of the decision they made on Sunday. I write something such as, "You prayed and asked Jesus to come into your life. That's the best decision you could ever make in your life."

3. Let them know you're praying for them, and if they have any questions, the church is there to help them. I want new believers to know that it's normal to have questions, and they don't need to have life figured out based on one church service. Instead, a group of loving people wants to help them take their first few steps of faith.

4. Invite them back to the church on Sunday. Engaging them in regular worship will aid in their spiritual growth.

5. Ask them to bring a friend. I usually add this as a postscript. This is important because if they invite a friend to attend with them, they are more likely to attend themselves. It also gives them an opportunity to talk to someone about the experience they had at church the previous week.

3. Cooperate

Our goal with new believer follow-up is to mobilize as many people to help as possible. One of the most important people to enlist is the person who invited the new believer to church in the first place. If you use promotional means such as direct mail or Google ads to attract people to your church, this won't be possible. However, if someone attends because a friend invited them, then we want that friend's help in the follow-up process.

A personal invitation is powerful. When someone invites a friend to church, they are using their relational equity to encourage that friend to attend. The church does not possess this credibility yet. The new believer's friend can pick up the phone and call because there's already a relationship established. Our goal is to enlist that friend to help the new believer take steps in their new faith. One way to know how the new believer was invited to church is to ask this question on the connection card.

How do we use the people who invited their friends to help us in the follow-up process? We do this by asking them to participate. We email them and let them know their friends decided to follow Jesus. Then we ask them to call their friends, congratulate them, offer to answer any questions they have, and invite them back to church on Sunday. We have found that our follow-up process is much more effective when the ones who invited them are involved in helping the new believers in their first few steps of faith, and the chances of seeing these new believers connect to our church goes up dramatically.

We tend to believe this kind of organic follow-up happens naturally. Unfortunately, it happens less than you think. The reason for this is that people often invite a co-worker or neighbor they don't know very well to church. Then, after the service, they don't have much contact with the person. This email informs the inviters of the decision that was made and the role they can play in the new believer's development.

4. Motivate

I want every new believer to take the next step in their faith. At Calvary, we mail a book called *Begin* to every new believer. This simple book shares the basics of the Christian faith. It's written in plain language, and it's a short read. My goal is to give new believers this gift so they can start to invest in their spiritual growth immediately. Too often, new believers are given nothing to begin their walk with God, or they are given resources filled with theological terms with which they aren't familiar. I regularly teach our Church Ninja members that there's nothing wrong with using theological terms, but you must define them simply for those new to the faith.

5. Educate

New believers need an environment in which they can grow and have their questions answered. This can be done in a new believers' class or a small group. There needs to be a place where we teach new believers the basics of the faith. In our new believers' class, we teach what it means to be saved, how to pray, how to get involved with Bible study, the need for fellowship, how to share their faith, where they can serve, and much more.

We live in a culture that is largely biblically illiterate, so if we want people to learn something, we must teach it to them. We can't simply say, "Go buy a Bible." Instead, we must explain the different types of Bibles available and recommend one to them.

Education should be presented alongside service. This way new believers learn and put their new knowledge to practice as they serve. I don't subscribe to the view that new believers will just pick up what they should learn along the way. Truth be told, most don't, and they end up as immature believers. Create a system for educating new believers and give them the tools they need to grow in their faith. Churches that train new believers have very loyal congregations with little division and few distractions that keep them from fulfilling the Great Commission.

6. Congregate

One common frustration of pastors is the irregularity of church attendance by those newer to the faith. What I have found is that few churches teach the importance of regular church attendance because they assume people are already educated about it. Unchurched people who give their lives to Jesus don't know believers should attend church weekly. In light of that, we emphasize the importance of congregating at a local church in three ways.

First, we teach it. As stated in an earlier chapter, the pulpit is the most powerful influencer in your church. We must use it wisely. Imagine the typical unchurched people who come to faith at your church. They've never attended church in their lives, but they visited your church, and they were saved on a Sunday morning. Then they start to attend church once every six weeks. Those of us in vocational ministry would say, "This person needs to get committed to God." However, the recent convert thinks, "I'm a Jesus freak! I went to church twice in the last three months, and I never went to church before."

This is why we need to teach the importance of making church a weekly habit and not assume that people will just "get it." We should do this from the pulpit, but we should also communicate this in our small groups, our new believers' classes, and any other environment in which new believers are listening.

Pastors suffer from something called "the curse of knowledge." I didn't make this up. This idea comes from Dan and Chip Heath's book, *Made to Stick*.[7] In the book, they present this scenario: You are drumming the beat to a song on a table with your hands, and you expect everyone to know what song it is. The problem is that no one guesses correctly. You don't understand it. You say, "Let me tap the beat again. This is so simple. It should only take you a moment to guess correctly." Sure enough, they can't figure it out. Why? They can't hear the song in your head.

This is the curse of knowledge. We know the song, but no one else can hear it. This is what happens in many churches. There's a song playing about what Christians should do, what they should say, how they should act, and how they should attend church. However, because new believers don't hear the song, they don't do what we hope they will. We must help them hear the song by laying out very clearly what we want them to do.

The second way to emphasize the importance of regular church attendance is to put church on their radar. This can be done in simple ways like emailing everyone in your database each week to let them know what's happening at your church on Sunday. Every Friday I send out an email to our entire church sharing what I will be teaching on Sunday. I also remind them to invite friends.

Lastly, you can help new believers develop a spiritual appetite. I have learned that people crave what you feed them. If you create an amazing environment in which they can grow in their faith and you help them take significant spiritual steps, church attendance won't be your problem. This is why we encourage people to bring their Bibles to church. We want to create a learning environment for believers each Sunday. My goal is to help create a hunger for God's Word in every attendee. When people have a hunger and thirst for the Word of God, you won't have a problem getting them to congregate weekly.

7. Demonstrate

We talk to new believers about demonstrating their faith when we teach them about baptism. Again, we cannot assume they understand the significance of baptism or even know what it is. We must explain it to them.

There are generally four barriers that keep new believers from publicly demonstrating their faith through baptism. If we understand these obstacles, we can help those who've stopped at the edge of the water to move ahead and obey Christ by being baptized.

Lack of instruction. You preach a message on baptism in which you teach its significance as a command of Jesus, and then you invite people to sign up for your next baptism. The numbers are much higher than for your last baptism, when you only made an announcement. What's happening here? You're helping people overcome a barrier to baptism without even knowing it.

Lack of instruction about the importance of baptism keeps many people out of the water. Many in your church would be baptized if you taught the subject more regularly. I encourage you to make sure this topic is in your preaching calendar. Provide a resource that answers the questions people might have about baptism. At our church, we put a copy of my book *Begin* in the hands of those deciding to be baptized because we want them to be fully informed of the decision they are making.

Tradition. Although I was baptized as an infant, I believe in adult baptism by immersion. In the city where I live, most people were baptized as infants, which is a barrier to adult baptism. How do we help people see the importance of adult baptism in light of their family tradition of infant baptism? My advice is to not pit the two against each other. Instead, I regularly tell people, "Your infant baptism spoke of your parents' faith. Now, by being baptized as an adult, you honor your parents because their hope when you were baptized as a baby was that you would follow Jesus. This new baptism allows you to decide to follow Jesus on your own." I don't fight people on the validity of infant baptism. I just encourage them to obey what the Scriptures command. The Bible says, "Baptism . . . now saves you, not by removing dirt from your body, but as a response to God from a clean conscience. It is effective because of the resurrection of Jesus Christ" (1 Pet. 3:21 NLT).

Opportunity. Often, people haven't been baptized because we don't offer baptism enough. I'm not a fan of a once-a-year baptism event. I know such occasions are exciting and high-energy, but I want to give people the opportunity to obey God *now.* I don't want to tell someone who wants to be baptized, "Great! We'll put you on our list for our next baptism in eleven months." Schedule regular baptisms so people can experience the joy of obeying God as quickly as possible.

Fear. "I'm not ready to be baptized." I've heard that phrase many times, and it's nearly always rooted in fear. Those who say it are usually afraid they aren't good enough, righteous enough, or holy enough to be baptized. How do we help them overcome this barrier? Our job is to tell them that the only requirement for being baptized is that they've made Jesus their Savior. Perfection isn't a prerequisite. Salvation and willingness to obey Jesus are.

Baptism is what separates the fans of Jesus from the followers of Jesus. It divides those merely playing church from those serious about spiritual growth and discipleship. It's an important step in the development of every believer. I make no apologies for challenging people to walk into the water. Our role as leaders is to help people become everything God wants them to be, and a big step in their development is baptism.

8. Assimilate

The quickest way to see sustained growth in your church is to develop an assimilation system that connects people to the church. By the way, I make no apologies for wanting people to attend my church. People do not grow in their faith alone. I also have no problem if someone decides to attend another church. That's their decision.

However, most people who stop attending your church usually stop attending church all together. We don't do anyone a service by leading them to Christ and then leaving them alone to figure out how to grow in the Lord. Instead, if God brought this person to your church, God has entrusted them to your care.

How do you assimilate people who have come to faith at your church? You need a follow-up process for first- and second-time guests. Clearly outline the next step for them, and create a system that leads them to follow that step. Here you can't fall victim to the curse of knowledge. The key for people to assimilate fully into the life of the church is by building relationships with others in the church, which can be done through small groups, special events, and your membership class.

How *Not* to Follow Up

There are four things not to do in your follow-up process. These things tend to scare people away rather than draw them into your church.

Don't Procrastinate

The number-one priority in our church office on Monday morning is following up with new believers. If you leave this for later, it won't get done. This is the most important follow-up you do, so put it at the top of your team's to-do list.

Don't Complicate

New believers need next steps that are clear and simple. If the next step we ask them to take is ambiguous or difficult, they won't do it. In addition, don't give them five steps. Give them just one and lead them through it. Fewer people will fall through the cracks.

Don't Suffocate

Give people space. Do your follow-up, but don't make people feel as though you're hovering. There's nothing wrong with emailing once a week—even twice a week if you have a good reason.

However, an email a day is irritating and counterproductive. Phone calls seem personal, but they can also intimidate new believers who have never spoken to a pastor. Remember, this is all new to them, so discern what permission you have to speak into their lives.

Don't Frustrate

Do what you say you will do. If you say you will mail something to them, mail it. If you say you will email them, make sure it happens. The last thing you want to do is make people feel as if they've been baited and switched. This is why I'm a big fan of doing all the follow-up on Monday. That way, people get their emails on Monday, and the books we told them we'd mail to them are in their mailbox by Thursday at the latest. The last thing I want is for someone to come back to church the following week and we haven't followed through on our commitments.

New believers are the most sacred trust a church can be given. Our responsibility before God is to help them take the next steps in following Jesus. My prayer to God has always been that our church will love new believers so much that he will send us many. Dealing with new believers is messy at times because they come to us with problems and hang-ups. They don't have it figured out yet, but there's no greater joy than seeing new believers take big steps in their faith.

7

The Three Irrefutable Laws of Outreach

Keith was one of those guys who made us wonder if he'd ever marry. It's not because he didn't want to marry. Instead, Keith was an awkward guy. He came to school the first day of our junior year wearing pink shorts, pink shoes with pink laces, and a pink shirt that read, "You can't touch this." With all due respect to MC Hammer, in the eleventh grade Keith had to "pray just to make it today."

Keith didn't try to blend in, nor did he do things conventionally. That's why when I heard the story of how Keith met his wife, I said, "That's the perfect Keith story." Keith went to Peru with a friend to vacation and have some fun. While at a nightclub one evening, he saw a woman whom he believed was the most beautiful woman in the world. He walked up to her and asked her to dance. She smiled but didn't respond. He grabbed her by the hand and spent the entire night dancing with her. At evening's end, Keith asked for her phone number, and he learned a truth that would limit most relationships: she didn't speak English.

I don't mean she spoke broken English or her vocabulary was limited. The girl didn't know a word of English. Nada. Through an interpreter, Keith got her contact information and flew home. He came back to the States with one mission—to learn to speak Spanish fluently. Keith, a kid who didn't know a word of Spanish that wasn't printed on a Taco Bell menu, became fluent in six months. Once he learned the language of his love, he flew back to Peru, swept his girl off her feet, and the rest is history. Marriage. Kids. Happily ever after.

Keith's story shares a fundamental truth with promoting your church to your community. Keith had to learn to speak his wife's language, and you as a church leader need to learn to speak your community's language. Churches promote their services and unfortunately see few results. The reason for a community's limited response is not because the church doesn't have great things to offer. It's also not that the people in your city are closed to the gospel. I've found that churches simply do not speak the same language as the community.

At first, leaders push back and say, "We don't use churchy language in our promotion. We know better than that." This shows that leaders are missing the point altogether. Leaders who feel frustrated when they promote their church are likely violating the three irrefutable laws of outreach.

In working with hundreds of churches, I've seen a few common mistakes about outreach. These mistakes are somewhat subtle. I myself have been guilty of transgressing these laws, and I've paid the price for it. Churches spend too much money and see too few results because they violate these laws.

Irrefutable Law of Outreach #1—Know Who You're Trying to Reach

The biggest mistake churches make with their promotional outreach is the erroneous belief that we, as leaders, can reach everyone. Most leaders agree intellectually that we can't reach everyone. In practice, however, we try to reach everybody and wind up reaching nobody. So few churches take the time to discover who God has gifted them to reach, and they inevitably make the costly mistake of seeking to attract everyone to their church.

As you can imagine, when you try to attract everyone, you end up attracting no one. When you realize God has uniquely equipped you to reach a specific group, there's no stopping your church's ability to reach them. As a bonus, you'll also spend a fraction of the cost reaching those you can reach. At Calvary, the average age of those in attendance is thirty-two, but that's not enough information to be effective in understanding who we reach. There are other demographics to factor in, such as gender, marital status, and where people live.

But factors below the surface are just as important. Psychographic considerations also give color to the outline demographic statistics provide. When I talk about this, the first question I usually get is, "What are psychographics?" Psychographics are how people think, their values, interests, and lifestyle. To understand Calvary, you must understand our psychographics. There's a common way we look at the world.

Let me give you a glimpse into the psychographics at Calvary that will shed some light on why this is so important. I am a second-generation Cuban American. That means my parents are Cuban and came to America seeking a better life. They left a brutal Communist regime, boarded a plane to the United States, and never looked back. I am the first person on my mom's side of the family to graduate from high school or college. I was born in Boston, so I am American by birth, but my heritage and upbringing were very Cuban.

At Calvary, more than 70 percent of our church is second-generation Hispanic Americans, Asian Americans, Haitian Americans, European Americans, and African Americans. When you dip below zip codes and marital status, our church is a place for people like me—people who are the children of two worlds: the world they lived in growing up at home and the world in which they were educated. This understanding influences everything. It influences how we view the world, our family priorities, even our politics.

Your church has a story. It's the common story of most people in your congregation. Until you discover what that story is, you will have a difficult time being effective in your promotional outreach. But once you crack the code, there's no stopping your church's ability to reach people.

Another important point to make is that every city has micro-populations. There are thriving churches in my city (Miami) reaching only first-generation Haitians; that's their target market. Many churches in Miami are committed to reaching first-generation Hispanics. Every element of their services is in Spanish—preaching, music, offering, children's and youth ministry. Some might argue that these are just various types of language ministry. However, let's move the conversation to a broader context. Every community has urban and suburban people. Every city has urban professionals and the urban poor. You must decide whom you are best equipped to reach and focus on reaching them.

As leaders, we love to recite the mantra that it takes all types of churches to reach all types of people. Do we really believe that? I don't feel any competition with the churches in my city. Nor should you. Instead, the only way we will reach our entire city is by every church focusing on those whom they are gifted by God to reach. When this happens, we won't feel the competition so many pastors feel. Instead, we'll be like an orchestra, all playing the same song but playing it in our unique way.

One question pastors ask me is, "How do I know who I'm best equipped to reach?" Although there are many ways to discover this, the basic rule is that you generally reach people like you. My wife and I started Calvary when we were in our midtwenties with no children. Guess who attended our church primarily? Singles and young married couples. Today, we have three children and we are quickly approaching forty. Our children's ministry is bursting at the seams and our church is filled with married couples with children. As your stage of life changes, so will your church. That's a fact. We simply must know that fact and use it to influence who we try to reach.

The purpose of our promotion is not to get a person to attend only one time. We can put together a promotional piece and attract many people to attend once. One benefit of knowing who you're trying to reach is seeing people attend for the first time who are also most likely to stay at your church.

It's not difficult to promote a special event and see many people attend. What takes more skill is promoting an event to the group of people most likely to attend your church. One reason churches have a big Easter and then drop back to their pre-Easter attendance is because they would rather have a crowd, but those who come are

87

not the ones that church is best equipped to reach. This is one reason outreach is so expensive for churches. Rather than zeroing in on a specific group, they feel the need to reach out more broadly. They lack focus on those most likely to attend and stick to their church.

Irrefutable Law of Outreach #2—Find the Message, Market, and Media Match

Master marketer Dan Kennedy called the message, market, and media match the "three-legged stool of marketing success."[8] Simply put, this marketing trifecta states that explosive success happens when these elements are aligned. The right message is put in front of the right market using the right media. With all due respect to Meatloaf, two out of three won't cut it in marketing.

I spoke with a pastor who had recently joined Church Ninja, my coaching program that simplifies church marketing and teaches pastors how to reach their communities faster and for a fraction of the price. He said he joined Church Ninja because he wanted to learn to use Facebook so he could reach young families.

As I asked this pastor about his church, I learned it is an older congregation with a rich heritage. However, they don't have any young families in their church. As we talked, I became increasingly confident that this church wasn't gifted in reaching young families. Yet, they were doing a very good job reaching empty nesters and seniors.

My counsel to him was to forget Facebook for the time being and start to advertise on the radio. He was shocked and told me no one listened to the radio. I told him, "I would agree if your church was full of people in the eighteen to thirty-five demographic. However, you lead a church full of people over forty-five, which means radio is your best friend."

If this pastor had put all his effort into Facebook ads, he would have reached some younger people. However, most of these people would not have stayed in his church because the church is not geared to young families or singles. The group listening to the radio would have attended if they were presented with an attractive ad, and many would have stayed because they would have seen a group of people just like them.

A friend created a radio ad a few years ago and aired it on the local rock station. He matched his message with the group that would listen to that station, and the result was a huge turnout for his Christmas outreach and sustained growth in his church.

This message to market to media match is true with radio, direct mail, Facebook, placement ads, and every other type of promotional outreach we do. At Calvary, we learned this lesson the difficult way a few years ago. We decided to do a big kickoff for our youth ministry, and we planned to promote it using direct mail. We had never done direct mail aimed toward youth, but we agreed to experiment and test it. Long story short, it was a disaster. We learned that direct mail is not a good way to reach youth. Online ads are much more effective. Even though we had a great message going to the right market, the media was off, which derailed our results.

As pastors, we believe the message should drive everything. The truth is that the media we use changes the amount of message we can share. You can try to fight this, but I promise you won't win. Instead, work within the borders you're given. Tailor your message to the market and each medium you use, and you'll see much better results.

Irrefutable Law of Outreach #3—Get People's Attention

A Church Ninja member called me recently because a resident in his city called to complain about a direct mail piece his church sent out. He asked if there was any way to stop this from happening. I asked, "Why would you want to do that? The fact that a few people get upset means people are paying attention to your direct mail piece. You should be having a party!" The worst thing that can happen to you isn't that people complain about your promotional outreach. Instead, the worst thing that can happen is that your outreach is ignored.

One big mistake many churches make is not focusing enough on the design of their promotional material to ensure that it is noticed. One benefit of Church Ninja membership is a free critique of your outreach pieces. We examine your direct mail or other promotion and show you ways to improve it. In reviewing hundreds of promotional pieces over the years, I've discovered that most churches fall victim to one of these design pitfalls.

Creating a Work of Art That Doesn't Communicate

One challenge pastors have is communicating to designers. The issue between these two groups is in how they view a design piece. The pastor wants to communicate information, and the designer wants it to look beautiful. The designer sees the words as clutter in the design.

Designers, allow me to set you free. No one will frame your art when you send it out. If you create a direct mail piece for a church, no one will pull it out of their mailbox and immediately insert it into a forty-dollar frame. It won't happen. Since that's the case, focus on presenting the information people need so they can decide about attending church.

Failing to Include Important Information

Designers like to work with as few words as possible because they don't see words as words. They see words as objects that should be placed somewhere. I have heard this from many designers. As pastors, we must make sure all the important information is on the promotional pieces we use. The bottom line: design is there to enhance the text, not replace it. Great design gives the text the best opportunity to communicate its message.

Using Design That's Too Busy

There's a general rule that people say no to what's confusing. If your promotional piece is difficult to read, people will not struggle to read it. Ensure that your design doesn't make the copy difficult to read, or your promotion will be a fruitless endeavor.

Making Something That Is Boring

I tell pastors all the time that everyone is allergic to boring. Some believe that simple means boring. I disagree. Simple isn't boring. Boring is boring. For example, clip art is boring. Here's a tip worth the price of this book: spend the money to get great images. Go to Getty Images or iStockphoto and buy the high-resolution images so your promotional pieces are impressive. There's nothing worse than getting a direct mail piece and seeing a blurry image with the copyright watermark in the corner.

Using Misspelled Words and Incorrect Grammar

Go out of your way to make sure your copy is conversational, but make sure your grammar is correct. It's not easy to do this and stay within the confines of a 5 x 7 postcard, but resist the urge to say, "It's good enough."

There's a reason writing is called "the merciless art." Make sure your copy is written well, and don't expect your designer to catch spelling errors. They aren't made for that. As I mentioned before, designers don't see words as words. They see them as objects that must be placed somewhere in the design. Assign someone to read your copy and make sure everything is spelled correctly. If something detracts from the message, then it's not a helpful design. So produce outreach pieces that honor God with the level of excellence that will get the attention of those you're trying to reach.

Kris saw a road sign that Calvary was having an egg hunt after our Easter services. He missed the Easter egg hunt the city had hosted, so he decided to visit Calvary and let his three children participate in the festivities. What he didn't plan on was hearing the gospel and God touching his heart. Within one month, his entire family had come to know Jesus as Savior. Today, Kris serves others as he uses his gifts to honor the Lord.

We recently recorded a video with Kris, and he said that one thing he loves most about Calvary is that when he walked in, we were speaking his language. Those in your community need you to learn their language and communicate the gospel in a way they connect with so they can respond as Kris did.

8

Offline Outreach Secrets

*M*inistry hurts. And I have found that the worst pains are self-inflicted. This is how I felt sitting at a stoplight near my house on the way home from church. We had sent out more than fifty thousand direct mail pieces to our community letting them know about a special Sunday service. Even after investing more than ten thousand dollars in promoting this event, only a handful of people attended.

I sat at the light feeling angry with myself and frustrated by my community. I was in the car alone but said aloud, "I'm done with direct mail because it doesn't work." I arrived home and grabbed Saturday's mail from the box before going inside. As I rifled through the pile, I saw a postcard from Banana Republic advertising a 40 percent off sale. I said to myself, "I don't want to miss this," and proceeded to put the postcard in my back pocket.

Then, as I opened my front door, it hit me: "Direct mail *does* work. I'm just not doing it right." This led me to discover which organizations use direct mail effectively and how we as church leaders can learn from them.

Here's how the story usually goes: A pastor moves to a new town to start a church. He calls a friend who pastors in another city and asks if he should do a mailer to launch his church. The established pastor says yes but then warns the church planter that churches receive only 0.05 to 0.1 percent return on that investment. That doesn't seem acceptable. Isn't there a better way? No business would use direct mail if that was the return on investment.

Before we go any further, let me tell you about our last direct mail campaign. We spent four thousand dollars and saw 221 newcomers attend as a result. How did this happen? It came about because of a series of changes I learned from the business community. We learned all we could, and the results were infinitely better than what most churches see. I learned that most churches commit what I like to call "the seven deadly sins of direct mail." The sooner you stop mailing this way, the more effective your efforts will be.

Direct Mail Deadly Sin #1—Trying to Mail to Everyone

Easily the biggest money-wasting mistake churches make is trying to send mail to everyone in their community. Although this sounds like a great idea at first, it's the primary reason churches get very few results in their direct mail efforts. You're not best equipped to reach everyone in your community. This is why we must be selective in who we mail to.

This is a tough pill for pastors to swallow because we believe everyone needs the Lord. The challenge is that we must be realistic about how God has wired us and who we are most likely to reach. I won't belabor this point since we covered it at length in the last chapter. What I will say here is that churches should work together. One way we do that is by focusing our efforts on reaching those we are most competent to reach. Once you know who you're most likely to reach, you must do the difficult work of finding where they are and thinking through how to reach them. Here is where demographics and psychographics come into play.

Direct Mail Deadly Sin #2—Failing to Segment Your List

Segmentation is getting a list of people—let's say an entire zip code of addresses in your community—and narrowing that list. If you want to waste tons of money, buy zip codes and mail to everyone on the list. If you want to be a good steward of the resources God has entrusted to you, then segment that list and eliminate the names of those you aren't gifted to reach.

At Calvary, we don't do a very good job of reaching seniors. It's not because we don't love seniors or want to see people come to the Lord in their later years. We're simply a young church, and we're best equipped to reach and minister to young people. So when we send direct mail, we mail only to homes that fall within a certain age range.

Although this might be disconcerting to some, I submit that we all draw the line somewhere. If you feel you should mail to everyone, where do you stop? Do you mail to everyone in your surrounding zip codes? Why stop there? Why not mail to your entire county or state? We all stop at some point. I'm simply asking you to focus on your immediate community and on those you can impact the most.

Besides segmenting a list of addresses in a given zip code, another way to build a mailing list for your community is to buy a list of names and addresses. At Calvary, we buy various lists at different times. According to the experts, 50 percent of the success of your mailings is due to the list, not the content.

To illustrate, I received a brochure from an organization I wanted to join. I had heard of the organization and didn't think I qualified, but when I read their material, I decided to join. They mailed it to me, so certainly they had ensured I was eligible. Turns out, I was not eligible to join the AARP (the American Association of Retired People) for another thirty years.

They should not have been mailing to me. I wasn't in their target market. Thus, sending me their material was a waste of money in postage, printing, and personnel. You can have the best copy in the world, but if it doesn't get into the hands of those most likely to respond, you will have limited impact.

Almost every person you want to connect with is on a list you can buy. Here are a few examples of lists we've purchased in the past: *Parenting* magazine subscribers, people who have recently moved to the area, everyone who's been divorced in the area in the last two years, subscribers to bridal magazines, those with a certain political affiliation. Your job is to decide where those you want to reach are listed and then buy that list to reach them.

The correspondence you get in your mailbox is a result of the lists to which you subscribe. You might not realize it, but companies sell their lists regularly, unless they specifically indicate they do not sell your contact information. This is a huge income generator for companies, and it's a great opportunity for organizations to get a list of qualified leads.

Imagine if we owned a company that sold sports memorabilia. We could start to mail catalogs at random to try to increase sales. Or we could contact *Sports Illustrated* and buy their subscriber list. Which would be more effective, a shot-in-the-dark mailing to random homeowners or a specific list of people who have spent money on sporting news? It's an easy decision. You buy the list.

This is also why *Sports Illustrated* can sell subscriptions for pennies. To them the money is in the list they build, not selling magazines. How does this work for churches? When we are going to begin a series of messages on relationships, we buy a list of everyone in our area who has been married in the last year. We also buy a list of everyone who subscribed to a bridal magazine. This way, when we send out our direct mail pieces, we know there will be a higher level of interest because of the subject.

I get *Hispanic* magazine in the mail. How? My best guess is I answered a phone survey in Spanish at some point, and I indicated I was Hispanic. Shortly after, the company who owns the magazine bought that list, and now the magazine arrives in my mailbox. If I were starting a Spanish church, I'd buy the subscriber list from them, segment the list based on my target age range and location, and start mailing to that list.

When you connect your market, message, and medium, you move from being an annoying pest to a welcomed guest. This happens when you segment and narrow the list. The key is finding the right people on each list and communicating via direct mail in a way that connects with them so they will give your church a chance.

Direct Mail Deadly Sin #3—Failing to Connect with the Reader

I teach our Church Ninja members the three-second rule: when your direct mail piece arrives in a mailbox, the average person will spend three seconds determining if reading your piece is worth their time.

My goal when I mail to our community is to get into people's "A-pile." What is the A-pile? When you get your mail, you lay it on the counter and separate it. There's the junk mail pile, the stuff that will be tossed out immediately. Then there's the A-pile, the pile of mail reviewed more closely. This includes bills, personal letters, magazines and newsletters you subscribe to, and unsolicited mail that captures your attention. Your goal is for your mail to resonate with your audience so they put it in the A-pile. To be accepted into the A-pile, you must focus your mailing so you can speak directly to your audience.

Television in America has learned this fact. There's a channel for everything. Thirty years ago, we had one sports channel: ESPN. Today, the sports genre has been sliced much thinner, and there's a channel for every major sport. This is the power of segmentation. It allows those of us who promote and advertise to speak with specificity and narrow our focus to those most likely to be interested in our message.

Let's be more specific. Let's say you have a big Mother's Day outreach. What do you do? You obtain several lists. You buy a list of every person who subscribes to *Parenting* magazine in your area. Then you narrow that list based on your geography and your other parameters. As I mentioned earlier, if you're speaking to parents, you can focus the copy of your direct mail to highlight the ministries of interest to families. This is the beauty of segmentation; it allows you to speak to people using language meaningful to them. I once heard a marketing master say, "If I only had ten thousand dollars to spend on a mailing, I'd spend five thousand obtaining the right list and five thousand mailing to them." But to make that mailing truly effective, you also have to be sure the message on your mailing resonates with those you're trying to reach.

Direct Mail Deadly Sin #4—Mailing Only Once

Once you narrow your list through segmentation, you can mail many times because you aren't mailing to as many homes. The typical church mailing process is to get a huge list with no segmentation of any kind (usually everyone in surrounding zip codes), and then mail a generic piece to everyone once.

This way is sure to spend lots of money and see horrible results. It takes more than one exposure for your community to notice you. That's why my recommendation is always to narrow your list and mail to it at least twice. If the day we promote is Easter or Christmas, we typically mail three times. However, two pieces in the week leading up to an event or a big Sunday is usually effective.

A common question I am asked is, "How soon before the event should we mail our pieces?" There's another issue involved here that I'll answer in a moment, but our philosophy has been to mail ten days before the event and then mail a second piece seven days before. If I were mailing three pieces, I would mail the first piece two weeks before the event, the next would be sent ten days before the event, and the last one seven days before the event.

Don't bother sending anything more than two weeks before your event. That's too far away to get on people's radar. Contrary to what some think, most people aren't very organized. Most people plan their lives week to week, which is why when you have a party you never get RSVPs until the week of the event. It's simply the nature of people. This is why political parties spend half their marketing budget starting two months before the election and blow the rest of their budget in the last two weeks. They understand the nature of people to forget.

The other question related to when to mail your pieces is, "How can I ensure that my pieces show up on time?" You can have the best direct mail piece in the world, but if it shows up late, it's useless. This is another reason you should do more than one mailing. To have yours delivered on time, you must know your local post office's delivery time. By law, the post office has fourteen business days to deliver your mail. In reality, they will probably deliver sooner than that, but you should factor these issues into your schedule.

Another important factor about direct mail is that bulk mail is the low man on the totem pole. Bulk mail pieces are mailed after all priority and first-class mail has gone out, which is why working with a mail house is so important. We never do a mailing without working with a mail house. They have a relationship with the post office. You should build a relationship with a mail house in your area and lean on their expertise when it comes to a mailing schedule. Ask them what their experience has been. They will usually err on the side of caution, so you probably want to take their advice.

Another important thing to do is to send a few mail pieces to different places you receive mail. Send a piece to your home, your office, and to another location in a different zip code. See how long it takes and plan accordingly. The last thing you want is for a piece to arrive late.

I received a direct mail piece from a church a few years ago advertising their Christmas services. The only problem was it arrived at my house on December 28. There's nothing worse than getting mail to someone's house late. Not only is it a waste of money, but it also annoys the people you mailed. Sometimes people underestimate the power of direct mail because they fail to do the simple things that increase its effectiveness.

Direct Mail Deadly Sin #5—Saying Nothing in Your Copy

A local church recently mailed a direct mail piece to our church office. It was a typical card and said nothing that would entice me to attend. It was boring, peppered with clip art of a sunrise that didn't copy well. It had the name of the church and the service times, but it never asked me to do anything. Some of these issues can be forgiven, but the biggest transgression here was that the postcard never asked me to attend the church, visit the website, or call the church. It apparently just wanted me to know the church was there. If you have bad copy, you're destined to have bad results. Copy matters.

Years ago, when the original Walkman was introduced, the ad for the product bombed and the company produced minimal sales. The typesetter reran the ad and made an error that turned the Walkman into a phenomenon. What was the typesetting error? It was the addition of a single letter. The original ad said, "Put music in your life." This wording was dead on arrival and did nothing for sales. But the second, "wrong" ad said, "Puts music in your life." The result was the Walkman becoming one of the best-selling items of the early 1980s. The addition of the *s* told the consumer what the product would do for them. This is the goal of good copy. It's supposed to tell readers the benefits of what you offer.

Benefits over Features

A marketing adage states, "People don't buy quarter-inch drill bits. They buy quarter-inch holes." People want the benefit of the item more than the item itself. Ironically, churches rarely talk about the benefits of attending. Instead, they talk about their church's features. Someone who doesn't attend church isn't interested in features; they want to know the benefits of attending.

What's the difference between features and benefits?

Feature: Batteries included.
Benefit: Ready to use right out of the box!

Feature: We have two services, at 10:00 a.m. and 11:30 a.m.
Benefit: Hear a message that will speak to your life at a time convenient for you.

Feature: We have a children's ministry during the service.
Benefit: Enjoy the service while our highly trained staff teaches your kids in a fun and engaging way.

Every direct mail piece needs a call to action. A call to action is the step you want the person to take because of seeing this postcard. It could be attending one of your services. It might be visiting your website. Whatever the step is, you must be clear in asking people to do it. A postcard without a call to action is a waste of money. Instead, give people a step to take. Tell them to attend your Father's Day service. Ask them to visit the link you've provided and reserve their gift. Don't create ads that lead people nowhere.

Most people have some level of fear or anxiety in going to an unfamiliar place. Most churches try to overcome the fear factor by saying, "We're very friendly." The problem is that everyone says that, so no one believes it. You must say something else that will get people's attention and help them put aside their worries. People usually have four questions when they attend a church:

What time are your services?

Where are you located?

How long are your services?

What should I wear?

When people log on to your website, they are usually looking for answers to these questions, which is why you should have all this information accessible on your home page. A "before you visit" page is invaluable for putting people at ease when they're thinking about attending. The key here is to know what their fears are and eliminate them with your content.

Use Understandable Language

I once received a flyer on my front door that advertised a church but used nothing but churchy language. It asked, "Are you tired of churches that don't talk enough about being washed in the blood? Churches that don't talk about being justified in the spirit and being sanctified by the Holy Ghost?" That flyer had so much theological language that you needed a Bible college degree just to understand it.

You won't reach people if you don't speak their language. The more you speak in terms the average person understands, the more you will connect with people. Instead of saying, "We're a church that preaches the true gospel without compromise," you might want to say, "We're a church where you can connect with God and learn more about him." There's nothing wrong with the former phrase; it's just that an unchurched person has no idea what that statement means.

Usually, contemporary churches think they have a leg up on traditional churches in this area. But I have found modern churches to be just as guilty of using insider terms when describing their church to outsiders. We use words such as *worship* in our copy, assuming that everyone knows that means music. Unchurched people don't equate worship with music. So when we write, "We have a relevant message and great worship," that doesn't mean anything to an unchurched person; try the phrase "great music" instead. We have to be careful about the words we use.

Be Clear

Years ago, I was the director of a Bible college, and we designed a beautiful catalog to attract new students. The reviews were glowing about how great the catalog looked and how it would attract hundreds of new students. Much to my dismay, weeks went by after we mailed the catalogs and we didn't receive one call. I was clueless about why this happened until someone pointed out that we had forgotten to put the phone number in the catalog.

I learned the important lesson that you must be clear in what you want people to do. If you want those in your community to attend your church, put a map on your postcard and tell how to get there. People say no to what is unclear, so I want every piece we produce to be very clear. This is my biggest problem with most church websites. Churches create cool names for every ministry in the church.

Unfortunately, if you don't have the decryption key, you'll never figure out where to go. The result of marketing and promotion is to get the recipients to visit your church, which is why we must make our copy clear and direct people with a call to action.

Direct Mail Deadly Sin #6—Not Tracking Your Results

Here's a typical scenario: A pastor joins Church Ninja hoping to learn how to reach his community. We talk, and he fills me in on the bad news that direct mail doesn't work in his area. I tell him that's a shocking statement and that I'll believe him if he shows me the data. This is the moment when the phone goes silent. I'll ask again, "Do you have stats to prove that?" He'll inevitably say that he's never tracked results. I let him know that I've had this conversation dozens of times, and no one ever has statistics because few know how to track their results.

I teach my Church Ninja members how to track their results on every direct mail piece they send. A simple way to track results is to create a unique URL for every mailer sent. If you do three mailings, create a URL for each mailing. If you're promoting Easter, you might create the URL www.yourchurch.com/easter. For the second mailer, you could make the URL www.yourchurch.com/easter13. The third piece could direct people to www.yourchurch.com/eastersunday. Then, as you check your website's statistics, you can see which URLs are getting the most hits. This way you can track the effectiveness of the media you're using.

At Calvary, we create a splash page that looks like the direct mail piece so people see continuity between the mailer in their hands and the website they visit. My favorite way to create unique URLs is to buy domains I can specifically use for mailing. You don't need to build an entire website for the domain; simply have the address forward to your main site. However, in your back-end analytics (tracking of traffic to your website), you will be able to see the referring address (how the visitor came to the page). This is a simple way to see the results of your direct mail efforts.

Direct Mail Deadly Sin #7—Not Learning from Each Campaign

You won't become an expert at direct mail outreach overnight. However, you are ahead of the curve simply by reading this book. You can learn from my mistakes and stand on the shoulders of someone who has gone before you. Not everything you try will work, but don't let that stop you from learning and testing new things. You have the benefit of learning from the testing we've done, but you'll also have to do your own tests and make your own discoveries. Try splitting your list. Create one type of piece for half your list. Then create an entirely different piece and mail that to the other half. See which performs better. Learn why it performs better and allow that to help you write and design better pieces in the future.

Jose and Lucy were looking for a church to attend with their two young sons. They received a postcard in the mail from a new church hosting a Christmas celebration near their home. They were busy during Christmas but wanted to attend the church, so they put the postcard on their refrigerator. It stayed there for most of a year. Even though it was far beyond Christmas, they attended and decided to call Calvary home. Today, their oldest son is integral to our staff, and they are pillars in our church. Direct mail is alive and well. We just need to leverage its power correctly.

9

Raising Money for Outreach

Money isn't everything, but it's right up there with oxygen.

Zig Ziglar

When I started Calvary Fellowship, we had no money, no members, and no facility where we could meet. The first night we met and the offering was twenty-five dollars, I realized the role money played in a successful church. Truth be told, I was afraid to talk about money. I have such disdain for the shenanigans I see on TV that I swore I would never be like *those* preachers. Instead, I did the opposite—I never talked about money.

In our church's first three years, I spoke about money once and I apologized through the entire message for talking about it. I went to the office the next day, and one of our pastors asked if he could speak with me. He came into my office and asked if tithing and sacrificial giving played an important role in my life. I said yes, giving was an important part of my life, and I would never stop tithing because I have seen God's blessings in my life over and again. He delivered a deathblow. He said, "If giving means so much to you and it's such a blessing, why do you rob our church of the same blessing by not talking about it?"

I was stumped. I never thought of it that way. I was so concerned with how a few disgruntled Christians would see me that I never even considered what most of the church was missing. This marked the beginning of my transformation about money.

One comment I hear from pastors who want to join Church Ninja or who participate in the discussion but don't act on what I teach is, "I wish we had the money to do what you teach us." I want to use this chapter to teach you lessons we've learned in raising money for outreach. You could use this system to raise money for anything in your church, but I will talk specifically about raising money for outreach. We've used these strategies to raise money for staff, equipment, missions, children's ministry, youth, and outreach and evangelism. Implementing this blueprint can also raise your church's monthly income as you raise the value of stewardship in your church.

A Theology of Stewardship

Many pastors have never studied money. Because stewardship is rarely studied in seminary or Bible college, most pastors know very little about money management, investing, cash flow, or budgeting. Every pastor should become an expert in financial areas because your church's health depends on it. If you don't believe me, talk to a church planter or pastor who has closed a church's doors. Ask them to give you five reasons the church closed. I can promise you lack of funding will be on the list.

The best book I have ever read about stewardship is *Money, Possessions, and Eternity* by Randy Alcorn. I encourage you to study this book and others like it to gain a solid understanding of stewardship. This way, you can lead your church with confidence in financial matters.

You can't run a church without money. It reminds me of young couples who say they'll live on love. That's great, but the mortgage company accepts only cash or checks. My lack of teaching on stewardship limited our church's ability to reach people, and it all came down to how I felt. As an arrogant twenty-six-year-old, I said, "If you don't want to give, then don't give. No one's begging for your money here. God doesn't need your money." God doesn't need it, but it certainly wouldn't have hurt a young church plant that didn't have two pennies to rub together.

Senior Pastor = Chief Fundraiser

There's no way to get around the fact that the church responds most to the senior pastor. This is especially true with financial matters. This means the senior pastor must shape the theology of stewardship in the church. It also means he must teach stewardship and cast the vision for funds that must be raised. This cannot be delegated to the finance person or the executive pastor. It simply won't work. The senior pastor is the person the church looks to for leadership.

Model Generosity

Pastors must model generosity to the rest of the church. Andy Stanley calls this being a "progressive giver," meaning we increase our personal giving each year. Too many Christians start to tithe and that amount is where their giving stays forever. As a pastor, you might not be the top giver in your church. However, no one should give more sacrificially than you should, which is a key to God's blessing. God blesses leaders who can be trusted.

When God isn't blessing a church financially, there are a few places to look for the cause. The stewardship system in the church is the obvious place. A bad system will produce bad results. If the system is sound, then it's time to look deeper. We must look at the giving of the key leaders in the church.

When a pastor doesn't tithe, God's hand of blessing is removed. When staff members don't tithe, God often will slow the blessing so pastors can note it. Pastors, staff members, and leaders must tithe for God's full blessing to be realized. God promises to "open the windows of heaven" to the person who honors him in tithing. Too often, the lack of resources is rooted here. God allows this to happen so leaders will deal with the problem of people not giving.

In my opinion, staff members who don't tithe should be released. Their lack of giving shows their lack of maturity and disregard for the church's mission. As with Achan in the book of Joshua, the sin must be removed from the camp for God's blessing to return.

Fundraising Basics

How does a pastor raise money for a specific outreach project? Here are four steps a church can take.

1. Emphasize a Specific Campaign

We do this often at Calvary. Even when our church was much smaller, we raised more than fifteen thousand dollars for direct mail for Easter and then did it again that year for Christmas. This is much easier when you've done direct mail before and you can say, "How many of you came to our church because you received a card in the mail?" These are the first people to give because they have experienced the power of promotion in their lives.

We have filmed videos with people who came to Calvary and ultimately gave their lives to Jesus because they received some promotion in the mail. When you connect media with life change, people will give sacrificially to support the project.

2. Make It Easy for People to Give

Do you remember the old days when church was simple? I don't, but I've heard it was simple. People came to church and put cash in the offering, which is how everyone gave. Then checks entered the scene, and later credit cards became a normal part of our lives. Now we are asked about automatic deductions and paying for services on a company website among the many other ways to conduct transactions in today's economy.

How has the church responded? Most churches only receive the offering on Sunday morning, hoping it's enough to cover all the church's needs and fund the church's vision. I contend that to have only one means of receiving tithes and offerings is a mistake. Instead, I encourage you to make it easy for people to give.

Many churches have several services so it's easy for people to attend. Many will open extra parking so it's easy for people to park. When it comes to giving, however, we receive Sunday's offering and that's the only opportunity people have to give. We do people an injustice and handcuff the church by having a single avenue of giving.

One secret to having an effective stewardship system is making it easy for people to give. Here are a few opportunities you can make available to your church:

The Sunday services. If you want people to be more likely to give on Sunday, put an offering envelope in the bulletin. This way, people feel as though that envelope belongs to them. Some churches put envelopes on the back of the chair or pew; that tends to be less effective because the average person believes those envelopes and everything else on the back of the pew belong to the church. If you take the time in your service to receive an offering, people are more likely to give.

The envelope. One thing we've done is make our offering envelope a business reply envelope, so if people aren't prepared to give on Sunday, they can take the envelope home, place their check inside, and send it in without having to find a stamp. This has been a very effective tool because it gives us an opportunity to mention it during our weekend services. We like to say that if they take the envelope and put a check inside, all they need to do is seal it and we'll take care of the rest.

Online giving. We live in an electronic world. It is important for the church not only to have a web presence but also to offer people the opportunity to give online. Companies such as PayPal have made setting up an online giving account very easy. This way, even if people are out of town or forget their checkbook, they can log on and give their offerings.

Online banking. Long gone are the days when it was commonplace for people to take their checkbooks with them everywhere. Instead, most people pay their bills electronically. We encourage people in our membership class and at other times throughout the year to add the church as a regular payee on their online banking. Then they can tithe online the same way they pay their power or water bill.

Auto-debit. Most of us have received information from our insurance company, phone company, or the bank financing our car payment that we can have our monthly payment automatically deducted from our checking account simply by filling out a form. We took that idea and created a form where a person could authorize us to deduct a specific amount each week or each month. This has been very effective for us, as people know they are being obedient in their giving. This also happens to be the method that most of our staff uses. What I love about this method is that it creates consistency in your church's budget.

Make it easy for people to support your church financially. A church where it is difficult to give will not be well resourced. Think through your systems and create opportunities for people to give. Your mission is too important to let finances stop you from succeeding.

3. Have a Follow-up System for Givers

I spoke at a church one Sunday, and my wife and daughter accompanied me. Carey was changing our daughter's diaper in the restroom when two other women walked in having a conversation about giving. The first woman, who had recently started to attend the church, was telling the other woman—presumably the person who invited her—about her first-time experience giving to the church. She said, "I don't get it. I gave five hundred dollars last week, and I don't even know if they received it. I'm not asking for a phone call, but at least a receipt in the mail showing that they got it would help. I know it was only five hundred dollars, but it's still something."

Several questions flood my mind. The first is, "When did five hundred dollars become an insignificant amount of money to give?" The second question is, "Is that woman likely to give again based on that experience?" My guess is that she won't give again, at least not anytime soon. Many people will stop giving if you have a poor follow-up system.

I give financially to a mission agency that follows up with me monthly. They send me a letter indicating how much I gave in the last month as well as my contribution total for the year. They also enclose a letter telling me how the resources will be used.

Here's the question that you should ask in your context: When people give at my church, what happens? Do they ever hear from us again? Stewardship follow-up is simple, but sadly there are very few churches that do it. When average people give at a local church, the usual response is silence. What does that silence communicate? It could communicate a lack of interest. It also creates questions in the mind of the person who gave. People wonder if the church got the check. They ask why they never got a thank-you. For many, giving for the first time is a step of faith. We would be remiss not to follow up, thank them for their gift, and let them know how these resources will be used.

Besides sending a thank-you letter when people give for the first time, it's also good to acknowledge when they become regular tithers. Reaching this point is an opportunity for the church to send a book or other resource that will encourage people for taking a step of faith and trusting God. In addition, when people give a particularly large financial gift, a follow-up phone call or card is very appropriate to thank them for their generosity.

4. Make Stewardship a Part of Discipleship

According to the Bible, stewardship is part of basic Christianity, which is why healthy churches train new believers to trust God with giving and challenge established believers to grow in their giving. Unfortunately, in some circles stewardship is labeled as something super-Christians do.

The simplest way to raise money for outreach is to teach people to tithe faithfully. The most effective way we have helped people is by asking them to take a tithe challenge. The tithe challenge is a great way to introduce churchgoers to giving and invite them to test God as Malachi 3 states:

> "Will a man rob God? Yet you have robbed Me! But you say, 'In what way have we robbed You?' In tithes and offerings. You are cursed with a curse, for you have robbed Me, even this whole nation. Bring all the tithes into the storehouse, that there may be food in My house, and try Me now in this," says the LORD of hosts, "if I will not open for you the windows of heaven and pour out for you such blessing that there will not be room enough to receive it.
>
> "And I will rebuke the devourer for your sakes, so that he will not destroy the fruit of your ground, nor shall the vine fail to bear fruit for you in the field," says the LORD of hosts; "and all nations will call you blessed, for you will be a delightful land," says the LORD of hosts. (Mal. 3:8–12)

A tithe challenge is a call for people to begin tithing for a specific period and to watch what God does in their lives when they give. We didn't invent the tithe challenge at Calvary; however, we have learned a great deal about maximizing its impact.

Although I could write an entire book on this topic, I want to briefly describe what we do. A typical tithe challenge at Calvary is ninety days. When I teach a message on giving, I reach the point in the message where I exhort the congregation to begin honoring God with their finances. I always share stories people have emailed me about what God has done in their lives when they took the tithe challenge. Then, when people show their desire to take the tithe challenge for themselves, we follow up with them by email throughout the ninety days.

Every Christian is a steward. The question is, are we good stewards? The Bible says, "Moreover, it is required of stewards that they be found trustworthy" (1 Cor. 4:2 NRSV). This is a requirement in the kingdom of God. We must teach financial stewardship yearly for two reasons.

First, there are people in our churches who are new and have never heard what God has to say about giving, saving, spending, investing, and debt. We do people a disservice by neglecting to teach this extremely important topic. Second, there are people in our churches who need to be reminded of what God has to say about stewardship. Our world bombards people with advertisements, sales, and zero-interest balance transfers on a daily basis. Teaching stewardship yearly is not too much. We all should be taught God's financial principles.

Today, hundreds of people attend Calvary because they clicked a Facebook or Google ad, received a postcard in their mailbox, or got a door hanger on their door. This was all possible because God's people believed that reaching others is important and that giving to support outreach is a worthy endeavor. Raising money for outreach is now part of our church culture, and it allows us to influence the culture around us.

10

How to Be the Billy Graham of Digital Evangelism

*A*shley is a college student who was chatting with a friend on Facebook one Saturday night. Ashley told her friend that she wanted to attend a church. When she hit the refresh button on her browser, our Calvary ad popped up on her page. She freaked out. She clicked our ad, got directions to our church, and less than twenty-four hours later attended one of our services and decided to call Calvary home.

Facebook is a phenomenon like no other on the internet. It has more than one billion users, and according to a Nielsen study, more than 50 percent of Facebook users log in each day.[9]

Facebook recently passed Google as the most visited site on the internet.[10] Nielsen also noted that the average person spends more time—up to seven hours a month—on Facebook than any other website.[11]

I like to ask my Church Ninja members a rhetorical question: If everyone most likely to attend your church visited the same coffee shop, would you advertise there? The answer is yes. That place exists. It's called Facebook.

Facebook has become a staple for Calvary to advertise our services, holidays, and special events. Our goal is to let everyone in our area know what we're doing and invite them to join us. As we begin to broach this subject, I want to give you four overarching principles about Facebook that will help you create ads that draw people to attend your church.

1. Great Ads Are Noticed

There is a science to creating a great Facebook ad. Contrary to what some people might think, the most effective ads aren't the most beautiful, artistic, or aesthetically pleasing. Instead, the best ads are noticed, period. In our experimentation and advertising on Facebook, we've discovered that advertisements are noticed for different reasons.

2. Great Ads Make a Strong Offer

I regularly see church ads on Facebook that don't contain a strong call to action. Pastors wonder why the ads don't produce more attendees. Great ads have a call to action that invites people to take the next step.

Politicians understand human behavior, which is why they ask for your vote when they speak to an audience. It seems counterintuitive for a politician to ask for the votes of those attending their rallies. Common sense dictates that the crowd already supports the candidate, hence their presence at the meeting. Yet, those who aspire to public office take nothing for granted. They know all too well humanity's ability to miss the point altogether. When politicians stand before a crowd, they call that crowd to action and ask them to go to the polls and vote.

Don't be afraid to make a claim. Tell people they will love your church. If they don't . . . well, they're the anomaly. Weak ads don't move people to do anything. Strong ads challenge people to take a step in your direction.

3. Great Ads Become Great through Testing

One thing we've learned is that great ads don't stay great for long, which is why you must keep testing and changing an ad's elements for it to stay strong. Monitoring your ad's effectiveness helps the ad get better. Slight tweaks can increase the number of clicks you receive and ultimately the number of people attending your church.

4. Great Ads Can Be Created for Any Group

It doesn't matter who you're trying to reach—young, old, married, single, male, female. Every group of people is on Facebook. For those who think Facebook is only for reaching the young, the largest growing segment on Facebook is senior citizens. They're getting online and connecting rapidly. My mom is in her sixties, and she has a Facebook account. My dad is in his midseventies, and he has a Facebook account. The issue isn't *if* the group we're trying to reach is on Facebook; the issue is *how* we will reach them.

Our job is to design a message that connects with the group we want to reach.

How do you create ads that attract people to attend your church? What's the secret behind effective ads? Three factors create an effective Facebook ad: the image, the headline, and the copy. This sounds easy enough, but I've learned from experience that it takes work to find the right combination of picture, headline, and copy to make a Facebook ad effective.

Target Your Audience

Before you build an ad to draw many people to attend your church, you must target who you're trying to reach. Although I discussed this at length in a previous chapter, I want to talk about how Facebook makes this easy for you. When you create a Facebook ad, deciding who you want to reach is determined by clicking a mouse.

Age, gender, and city are all basic decisions in Facebook ad creation. What's great about Facebook is you can clone the same ad and test it against different demographics to see which group responds best. The key to being successful on Facebook is to narrow your field and be laserlike in your focus, knowing who you're trying to reach. This isn't easy, because as a pastor you want to reach everyone. However, you must have a sober mind and know who God has gifted you to reach. Once you determine your target audience, you must create ads that will appeal to this group.

Use Attention-Getting Images

Here's the secret few people know about Facebook: an image sells the ad. The image accounts for 85 percent of a person's decision whether to click on the ad, because the image gets people's attention. What images stick out and get attention?

Unusual images. A health-related ad uses a picture of two eggs sunny-side up. It's effective for many reasons, one being that it's unusual because you don't expect to see a picture of eggs on Facebook.

Loud images. Many successful ads use bold text with a dark background. This is simple and not very pretty, but it gets the job done when trying to get people's attention.

Female images. The statistics are overwhelming that images of women perform better than images of men. This statistic is true with both men and women. People in general find a picture of a woman more appealing than a picture of a man. I'm not talking about sexy pictures or things we'd think are inappropriate. A close-up of a woman smiling gets more clicks than a picture of a man smiling.

We tested this theory at Calvary with a free report we gave away called "The Foundation of a Successful Relationship." We ran two ads. The first was a close-up shot of a smiling young woman in her twenties. The second was a close-up of a smiling young man in his twenties. We ran both ads for three days. The results were astonishing. We got 171 clicks with the woman's picture compared to 21 clicks with the man's. Women win on Facebook ads.

Ugly images. A Christian publisher ran a hideous ad a few years ago inviting people to enter to win a free library. The image was bright green and pixelated. It looked like a low-resolution image, and inside the bright green box in white letters, it said, "Win a FREE Library." Although I have forgotten 99 percent of the Facebook ads I've seen, I'll always remember this one because it stuck out. It was ugly, it drew my attention, and I clicked.

Button images. In their design, button images present a call to action. This happened to me recently. I was on Facebook and saw an ad for a World War II movie I wasn't interested in seeing. But I saw the button image and I clicked anyway.

Clear images. People don't click an ad if they can't see what the image is. The trouble with adding an image to Facebook is that the pictures we want to use are usually much larger than the hundred pixels to which they are shrunk. Although an image might look great full-screen on your computer, it can become indecipherable once it is added to your advertisement. Test to make sure the image is clear or your ad will suffer.

There are several images you should never use. Never use a picture of your church's home page. It looks terrible, and it's so unimaginative.

Don't use an image if its shape is distorted when it's added to your Facebook ad. It loses the intended effect.

Don't use images with small text. If people can't read the text, they won't bother clicking the ad.

Don't use images that take only half the space allotted in your ad. It looks terrible, and the results are not good.

Also, make sure you have the correct license to use an image. Not everything on iStockphoto or other stock photography sites have licenses for multiple-use advertisements. Double-check your photo agreement. Photos of people from your church can only be used if they sign a waiver. Copyright law is an extremely important set of guidelines to follow. If you're unsure, check with an attorney or copyright licensing specialist.

Use Headlines That Connect

A good headline enters the conversation people are already having in their minds. What question are people in your community asking about church? Either ask that question or answer it in your headline. One of the best headlines we've used says, "A Church That Makes Sense," because often unchurched people think church doesn't make sense.

The key to writing a good headline is to address the issues important to readers. I recently saw a church ad on Facebook with a headline that read, "Come Help Us Grow." That should receive the worst headline of the year award. You don't begin a relationship by asking something of the other person. Instead, think how you can heal a hurt, meet a need, or answer a question.

The best response we've ever received for a Facebook ad was an Easter ad with the headline, "Find Hope This Easter." It was very simple with a purple Easter egg as the image, and the results were amazing. Clear beats out cute every time.

Letting people know you're a church will probably get you more clicks than pretending to be something you're not. We've learned that if you take people's major objections to church and turn those into positive headlines that answer the objections, it works out great. You hurt your advertisements when you're unclear, try to be cute, or use lingo that doesn't make sense to someone outside of your church.

Use Copy That Attracts

Make your copy brief. You only have 25 characters to work with in the title and 135 characters in the body text. That's less than one text message. It's not much to work with, which means you must get to the point and make every word, letter, and punctuation mark count. The key to writing good Facebook copy is to promise to deliver one thing in your ad. In addition, the answer should come when they click your ad.

This is the number one reason churches don't see more people attend their services after clicking their Facebook ads. People click an ad for a church and are sent to the church's home page. Once they're on the home page, they don't know what to do, so they leave and move on with their lives. What's worse is that now you've wasted money, and next time those people probably won't click your ad.

When we promote a big event at Calvary, we create a simple landing page that explains who we are and what event people are invited to. We do our best to make the language and look of the ad match the landing page. This page will answer the questions people have about the ad they clicked, and it gives them a sense of continuity from the ad to our main website should they decide to check it out.

Secret Facebook Stuff

Advertise Thursday through Saturday. This simple tip will save you this book's cost a hundred times over. You can advertise daily, but you won't get the most bang for your buck as you will by having your ads only run Thursday through Saturday. You want to spend your resources on the days when people are most likely to click and then attend.

Advertising later in the week is better because people forget most of what they see within seventy-two hours. People will remember your church the closer to Sunday they click. People who click your Monday ad are far less likely to attend your weekend services than those who click on Friday or Saturday night. We advise you to turn your ads off Monday through Wednesday and turn them on Thursday through Saturday. This will save you the resources you would have invested early in the week and will let you raise your daily advertising allowance for the more strategic days.

Buy clicks, not impressions. I firmly believe in paying per click, not by impressions. Just because an impression shows up on a screen doesn't mean the person sees the ad. However, because it's an impression, you still must pay for it. Another reason this strategy works great is because Facebook stops running ads that perform very well. Once they see that an ad has received many clicks, they bench the ad for the rest of the day to make room for other ads. The only way to combat this is to pay by click.

When you buy clicks, Facebook isn't paid until people start to click. Facebook has a strong financial incentive to show your "pay per click" as much as possible. They will show your ad until you reach your daily spending limit. We've learned that when you pay per click, you get just as many impressions anyway.

Watch your radius. When you create a Facebook ad, the default is to show your ad to the cities in a radius of ten, twenty-five, or fifty miles. We recommend that you uncheck the radius box and manually add the cities where you want your ad seen. I'm in Miami, but twenty-five miles away is almost to Palm Beach County. There's little chance that anyone will drive through two counties to attend our church. Therefore, we uncheck the radius box and manually input different towns and cities we want to target. Doing this gives you much more control over who you reach. You know your community better than Facebook does. With a bit of extra effort, you can target the cities and towns of those most likely to attend your church.

Make an appropriate bid. Most churches pay too much for their Facebook ads. I once got a call from a new Church Ninja member who was paying $2.50 a click. I nearly fell out of my chair when he sent me his statistics. We have never paid more than $1.00, and usually we're under $0.60 a click.

I looked at his ad and noticed that he had two ads going out to the same group. I explained to him that this was driving up the price because he was bidding against himself. Once he removed one ad, we researched his remaining ad and showed him some strategies to lower his ad costs.

One tip we gave him was in his bidding. When you first place an ad, Facebook has a suggested bid for the ad. I always place the ad and set my maximum bid at the suggested bid to get the ad shown. The little-known secret is that Facebook rewards ads that perform well by lowering the ad rate. I recently ran an ad where the suggested rate was $0.80 per click. I bid $0.80 and started to run the ad. The ad ran so well that I noticed my pay-per-click price dropping. Therefore, I lowered my bid to $0.40. When the ad was at its best, I paid $0.30 a click.

Facebook's goal is to create the optimal user experience. If people like your ad, Facebook will lower your price as a reward for creating a great user experience for Facebook members.

About bids, I would add that you should bid only odd amounts. When I have a new ad, instead of bidding $1.00, I bid $1.03. This way if I bid against someone who bids only $1.00, my odd-numbered bid will win. I have done this hundreds of times with my church and dozens of other churches, and I have found that bidding odd numbers gets your ad shown while other ads wait on the bench.

Always be testing. We are always testing at Calvary. Our goal is to create the most effective ads possible. We test ads by creating competing headlines with the same image and copy to see which performs better. We will run different images with the same headline and copy to see which is superior. We will test ads with variations on the copy with the same headline and image to see which gets more clicks. We are serious about testing because we know that we can be close to a great ad, and all it takes is a little tweak to get it there. The great thing about Facebook is that testing is so easy. You simply create an ad and use some existing features of the old ad.

Know what you can and can't do. One of the most common mistakes churches make on Facebook is trying to do too much. Facebook gives you very few characters to work with, so you must be specific in your objective. Facebook is not the place to explain your statement of faith, your unique philosophy of ministry, or your church's history. Facebook *is* a great place to encourage people to click your ad and invite them to a service at your church.

Some think Facebook doesn't work as an outreach tool, but their trouble is they're trying to get Facebook to do something it wasn't designed to do. It's like cutting a steak with a spoon. Spoons are great, but not when you're trying to cut a New York strip. You have to use the right tool for the right objective.

With one Facebook ad, you can share your message with more people than you will preach to in an entire year. For this reason, Facebook can become the greatest evangelist in your church as you execute effective ads. Countless "Ashleys" in your community are looking for a church to call home, and Facebook can help you reach them.

11

The Practical Field Guide
to Explosive Outreach

*I*t's easy to get to the end of a book like *Pull* and feel over-whelmed. We've shared much information as well as many strategies and tips on how to use all available means to reach people far from God. Yet, despite all that's been shared, questions can linger. I've devoted this chapter to answering the questions that keep churches from stepping out and using all the opportunities available to reach people.

We're a church that wants to reach unchurched people, but we lack resources. How can we implement the strategies you've outlined in *Pull*?

Every church has limited resources. All churches must use their resources wisely and be good stewards of the funds entrusted to them. Having said this, a church with limited funds can still do plenty of outreach.

If a church can't afford to do direct mail, I challenge them to print door hangers instead. As I tell our Church Ninja members, door hangers are just like direct mail. The only difference is you must be the postman.

Many strategies we've outlined in *Pull* don't cost anything except some time. If you can't buy Facebook ads, then mobilize your church to invite everyone they're connected with, and you can still reach people using Facebook. Too often, finances are the excuse leaders use to do nothing related to outreach. My advice is to do what you can and watch God bless your efforts.

Where do I begin to develop an outreach strategy?

The most important place to begin developing your outreach strategy is knowing who you're best equipped to reach. I recently got a phone call from a Church Ninja member about to sign a contract with a marketing company. He called to ask my opinion, and I told the pastor not to do it. When I asked him why he wanted to enter into a contract with them, he said, "But the salesman told me it's a good deal."

Here's the challenge in that response: I believe that the salesman was giving this pastor a good deal. However, if this form of media doesn't get your message in front of those most likely to respond to it, then it becomes a very bad deal. Instead, you should begin from the place of knowing the group God wants your church to reach and using your best resources to reach them. Once you know who you're trying to reach, simply follow the strategies outlined in *Pull*, and you'll be well on your way to seeing lost people found.

Calvary Fellowship started as a home Bible study with five people. The most daunting task we had early on was figuring out how to let people know we existed. I made the mistake of putting all our hopes in one method rather than using different means to communicate who we were as a church and the gospel's message.

I see churches make this mistake all the time. They think Easter will attract enough new people to keep the church growing throughout the year. Or they are "old school" in their thinking, believing personal evangelism is all that matters and all we need. The key is to take great action and do several things simultaneously. Use every means of communication available to let your community know that your church exists so you can introduce them to the God who is willing to forgive their sins and change their lives.

How should a church focus on making its presence known?

Mini-Easters. These are the natural high days of the church calendar. Some days, such as Easter and Mother's Day, are built into the calendar. Other mini-Easters can be created throughout the year to build momentum and get new people to come to the church for the first time.

Personal evangelism. Nothing can substitute for people sharing their faith with family, friends, co-workers, and classmates. However, for people to share the gospel message that has changed their lives, they must be equipped with the tools to do so.

Excellent weekend services. To the average person, your church is reduced to one hour on Sunday. The sooner you start to take Sunday more seriously, the better off your church and your community at large will be.

Promotion. Personal evangelism is how we reach out to those connected to someone in our church, but how do we reach out to those who have no connection whatsoever to our church? The answer is promotion.

What's a good budget to allocate for outreach?

There are two key issues with budgeting for outreach and marketing. The first is having a yearly budget. The second is having a budget for each event. It's impossible for me to tell you what you should budget for outreach, because I don't know your individual situation.

What I encourage you to do is see every dollar you spend on outreach as an investment, not an expense. At Calvary, we budget close to 10 percent of our annual budget for outreach. This includes direct mail, Facebook and Google ads, invitation cards, and any other promotion we decide to do.

Some pastors like to use billboards as a wow factor in the community. I get a fair number of questions about billboards, so I'll share my thoughts here. Billboards tend to be very expensive. A billboard in Miami runs anywhere from five to ten thousand dollars for four weeks. We've had billboards, and they've done well, but it's not strategic to spend your entire budget on billboards. Billboards are considered reminder advertising. When large companies such as Coca-Cola, Pepsi, McDonald's, and Burger King have invested their ad dollars in other media, if funds are left over, they buy billboards.

The other challenge for churches using billboards is that we are usually promoting a particular Sunday. When you buy a billboard, your event will often occur before your billboard rental has elapsed. An Easter billboard doesn't help you the week after Easter.

Instead, when you use Facebook, for example, you set your daily budget high, and then you create ads that will connect with people.

You do direct mail so your pieces hit the mailboxes at strategic times before the event.

A final factor to note about billboards is that these days no one looks at them. People are texting rather than looking at the road. If they don't even look where they should when they drive, they certainly don't stare at billboard signs on the road.

Are there particular topics I should preach yearly?

Imagine a typical South Florida day. Not a cloud. Ninety degrees with about 100 percent humidity and traffic as far as the eye can see. I was driving to work one morning, and while sitting at a stoplight, I saw the car in front of mine start to emit an ominous white smoke. When the light turned green, every car moved except mine. It wasn't the car in front of me acting like a chain smoker; it was mine. What happened? I neglected to change the oil, and my car's health suffered. I had to replace the entire engine because of my neglect. An oil change costs $30, yet my negligence cost me $1,700. I'm not an investment guru, but I'm sure this was not a good use of money.

Just as your car needs regular maintenance every three thousand miles, there are topics you as a pastor should return to every twelve months to keep the church healthy. At Calvary Fellowship, we have a list of topics we add to our preaching calendar yearly without fail.

Servanthood. We include messages on servanthood for two reasons. First, as a portable church doing several weekend services, we need a large pool of volunteers to make our weekly services happen. This includes setup and teardown crews, children's ministry workers, several worship teams, and many other areas. As the pastor, you are the chief recruiter of new servants in the church.

Second, servanthood is a core distinguisher of a follower of Jesus. It is the defining characteristic of greatness in God's sight. "Whoever wants to be great must become a servant" (Matt. 20:26 Message). If we desire to see those in our churches live lives of greatness, then servanthood is the path that leads them there. A healthy church is one in which people serve others for Jesus's sake.

Stewardship. Every Christian is a steward. The question is, are they being a good steward or not? The Bible says, "Moreover, it is required of stewards that they be found trustworthy" (1 Cor. 4:2 NRSV). This is a requirement in the kingdom of God.

Teaching yearly on stewardship is not too much. The average person sees as many as five thousand ads a day.[12] There are people in our churches who must be reminded of what God has to say about stewardship. We all should be taught God's financial principles.

Also, new believers have never heard God's financial principles taught. We do people a disservice by neglecting to teach this extremely important topic.

Relationships. If you have many married couples in your church, teach about marriage yearly. If you have a large population of singles in your church, teach about single relationships. I would still teach on marriage in largely single churches; I would just make the series shorter. Singles are very interested in marrying, so the information you share about marriage will have plenty of relevance to them.

If your church is like mine (and I'm guessing it is), you have couples who struggle in their marriages. Most couples don't know God's purpose for marriage, let alone how to handle conflict or how to communicate, which is why we should teach these principles every year. Couples who heard last year's marriage series will be happy to hear another series because chances are they had conflict in the last twelve months and could use the reminder.

Evangelism. This core purpose of the church is the one that will quickly fade if not focused on regularly. Most Christians (at least those who don't have evangelism as their primary spiritual gift) must be reminded that theirs is a lost world, and God has called us to reach others in the Holy Spirit's power.

We uphold the value of evangelism by giving people an opportunity to receive Christ in our services, by creating a Sunday environment in which people want to invite their friends, and by giving people the tools to share their faith with those around them. If we say, "People have heard the Great Commission before. I'm sure they get it," we are unintentionally lowering the evangelistic heat in our church. Churches that are white-hot with evangelistic zeal are those teaching, modeling, and celebrating evangelism!

Other topics might be very important for your church to teach yearly. The key here is to identify them and make sure they are on the calendar, so your church doesn't seemingly "break down" in any area of mission, vision, or ministry.

Bob, you preach messages that are expositional and evangelistic. How do you preach to disciple believers and reach the unchurched simultaneously?

I get this question regularly. The reason is that many people who teach the Bible verse by verse don't seem to reach people far from God with this style of teaching. On the other hand, most pastors who take evangelism seriously primarily teach topically and believe this is the best way to reach unchurched people.

This question hits on two things very important to me: preaching verse by verse through the Bible, and reaching people far from God.

By answering this question, I must deal with a misconception—that expositional preaching is primarily a tool to reach believers and topical/felt-needs preaching reaches unchurched people. I don't buy this idea. I am thankful to the Lord that we've seen more than one thousand new believers at Calvary in the last year, and the entire time we've preached through books of the Bible verse by verse.

The key to expositional teaching that connects with unchurched people is to teach with a point, working through a section of Scripture, explaining the meaning and giving relevant application.

Expositional teachers have an advantage over primarily topical teachers: Unchurched people sit and watch us work through a chunk of Scripture, and they say, "That's what the Bible says." The purely topical teacher hops around and pulls a random verse here and there, and the unchurched person wonders if that's what those verses mean because they aren't used in context. I'm making generalities, but the point is that teaching through a whole chapter or even a paragraph of Scripture assures the listener that there's no "funny business" happening with the text as it's preached.

For me, I am sold on teaching the Scriptures verse by verse (although some subjects are better handled in a topical manner) because it's the best way to disciple a congregation. Moreover, it's a great way to reach unchurched people who are skeptical about the Bible.

Preaching is so important because you shape your church's culture with every message you preach. Most pastors don't realize this early on. They get a good idea and execute it. Another good idea comes along, and they put it into play. Next thing you know, two years have passed and you've unintentionally created a culture in your church.

Instead, be intentional about your messages. Look at your entire calendar yearly and see where your preaching schedule needs work. Are you preaching too many messages to attract? Balance that with a few book studies through the Bible. Been spending a lot of time teaching Daniel or Revelation? Talk to your congregation about marriage and family for a few weeks. One reason I teach expositionally is that it creates a culture in our church in which the Bible is valued. People don't need my advice. They need God's Word. Examine your preaching and your preaching calendar carefully, because they create the culture your church will become.

I've been told direct mail is dead because everyone is online. Why do you believe otherwise?

To answer this question, allow me to share some statistics from a 2008 DMNews/Pitney Bowes survey that might encourage you to delve into the world of sending out direct mail for your next big Sunday at church.

People who sort and open their mail daily: 85 percent

People who say they are examining their mail more closely for coupons and other special offers and events: 67 percent

People who say they tried a new business because they received direct mail from them: 40 percent

People who renewed their relationship with a business because they received direct mail from them: 70 percent[13]

You can reach many people through direct mail if you do it right. Follow the steps outlined in chapter 8, and you will see results far above the average results most churches see.

You're a big believer in keeping good data. What are the most important statistics to keep track of when determining a church's growth and development?

We know what numbers such as 98.6 or 120/80 mean—they're gauges of our physical health. Likewise, we look at gauges on the dashboard to see if our car is "healthy." If something lights up or goes into a red zone, we know there's a problem.

In the same way, churches have metrics—numbers that speak to the health of the body of Christ or to our need for help. The Bible says, "Know well the condition of your flocks, and give attention to your herds" (Prov. 27:23 NRSV). What are the metrics that can strongly indicate the health of a local church body?

I look to the following seven vital signs that speak the language of health or help. One could argue that plenty of other metrics are valid for a church, and I would agree. But just as your car's dashboard gives you the most critical information about the health of the engine, these seven metrics will be some of the most important indicators of your church's health, helping you see where attention and energy should be applied.

Five first-time guests for every one hundred attendees. Simply put, churches grow because of first-time guests. To measure at what rate your church can grow, see how many first-time guests you have each weekend. As a rule of thumb, a good goal is five first-time guests for every hundred people in attendance. This will tell you what the evangelistic temperature is at your church. (Note: Just to stay even, because of natural attrition, you typically need at least three first-time guests for every hundred attendees. You need five if you actually want to grow.)

One baptized for every three decisions. Not every person who makes a decision for Jesus by walking forward, checking a response card box, or raising a hand in a service will go on to take the step of baptism. Many factors can keep a person from taking that step, but a healthy proportion of new believers should understand the significance of baptism and go into the water to declare their faith publicly.

When a pastor regularly teaches about baptism, providing resources to help people overcome mental barriers to it and giving opportunities to take that step of faith, people will be baptized. How many? A good metric is one out of every three who make a recorded salvation decision.

Over the years, when I've been negligent in teaching baptism, the number of baptisms has declined considerably. Therefore, I watch this number to help me make sure I regularly communicate this command of Jesus.

This week's attendance compared to this week last year. One big mistake I made early in ministry was to gauge how our church was doing weekly. Was attendance better this week than the week before? This measuring can become a roller coaster that drives a pastor crazy. If our weekly numbers are up, we feel good. If they're down, we call ourselves losers all the way home from church. Countless factors can bring weekly changes in these numbers.

We get a better picture of what's happening in our church by comparing this week's numbers with the same week last year. This gives us the metrics we need to measure health. For example, comparing attendance from this Labor Day weekend to Labor Day last year will tell you more about your church's health than comparing each weekend in September. And because Easter moves around so much on the calendar, always compare this Easter with last Easter rather than with that same Sunday from last year.

Current giving compared to the same period last year. Likewise, don't measure giving on a weekly basis, because giving fluctuates from week to week for many reasons. When seeing trends, look at the bigger picture. Compare this quarter with this quarter last year, or compare all this year with all last year (or previous years). This will give you a much better picture of your church's condition.

Fifty percent involved in ministry. For believers to grow to maturity, they must experience both input and outflow. Many Christians are very good at receiving, but for the sake of spiritual development and maturity, churches must emphasize the importance of learning to serve and give.

When a church has 50 percent of the congregation mobilized for ministry, it's a sign of health. What does this ministry involvement include? At Calvary, we define it as "serving someone else in the local church for at least one hour a week." This could be serving at one of our weekend services, hosting or leading a small group, or being involved in some aspect of the church's outreach or evangelism.

Thirty percent committed to membership. A church that has 100 percent of its people committed to membership is not a healthy church. That might sound like heresy, but follow my thought. Churches should always have a healthy-sized group of new believers in the crowd. Weekly, there should also be people in attendance who aren't even Christians yet and who are considering the claims of Christ. If a church has less than 30 percent of its attendees going through its membership class, it's a light on the dashboard indicating that something's awry.

This problem could be solved by something as simple as making more effective announcements about the membership class or preaching membership more regularly. Or the solution could be more involved, such as giving the membership class a better format and more dynamic appeal.

50-30-10-10. No, this isn't a code for less expensive long-distance rates. It's a guideline for budgeting. Since day one at Calvary Fellowship, we've sought to attain these four percentages for our financial resources:

Staffing: 50 percent

Operations and ministry: 30 percent

Missions/Outreach/Benevolence: 10 percent

Savings: 10 percent

We haven't always operated exactly at these levels. At times, we've been higher on staffing (which is typical for new church plants), or we've not saved a full 10 percent. But the 50-30-10-10 split has been our overall operating framework.

Where does membership fit in your follow-up process?

Formal church membership is something I struggled with early in my ministry. I believed the church differed from American Express, where membership has its privileges, so I shied away from any membership process. Instead, I told all attendees they were members of Calvary Fellowship if this was their church home. The results of that decision were disastrous.

It was not the kind of poor decision making where you see the consequences immediately. Instead, it was a gradual repercussion, like slowly neglecting your health. I believed that a loose definition of membership would not be a detriment to the church, but it certainly was. The lack of a strong membership process kept the church in a weakened state. To remedy this, we instituted a formal membership process at the five-year mark of our church's history. The results have been astounding.

Set the Bar High

I have become a firm believer in membership, and I am a proponent of setting the bar high as we communicate expectations to potential members. Most churches tend to do the opposite; they set the bar low at membership and then seek to turn up the heat as time goes on. You should turn the heat up from the beginning because the way a person joins your church is the way he or she will stay. If you ask for little commitment, I can almost guarantee the member's commitment will be weak.

We have potential members sign a membership covenant stating what they commit to uphold and do as a member of Calvary Fellowship. The covenant involves small group participation, regular church attendance, faithful giving, reaching the unchurched, and serving in the church. We don't apologize for setting a high standard. Instead, we confidently share what the commitment level is and invite those willing to collaborate with us to join.

Keep Members Accountable

A mistake some churches make is that they outline the require-ments of membership but never follow up to see if members follow through on their commitment. Leaders who do not follow up on members are doing members a great disservice. Why ask people to sign a covenant saying they will uphold particular values and then never check whether they do? We have found that a review of our members is a great way to discover pastoral care needs in a member's life.

For example, if we see that members haven't served in any church area for some time, we call them and ask if something is keeping them from serving. Often, we discover a family member has become ill, has experienced increased pressure at work, or even has a strained marriage relationship. When we have checked the financial giving of members, we have sometimes seen that a member has stopped giving. Again, a simple phone call can reveal a financial crisis, and the church can then help the family financially or through financial counseling. This tool has greatly helped us in caring for those in our church.

Decide What Commitment Means

Ask any ten people what commitment to a local church means, and you will get ten different responses. Membership has a way of setting the baseline of commitment. If you don't teach what regular church attendance means, everyone will decide for themselves. If you don't teach what faithful giving is, people will create their own definitions. A healthy membership system sets the biblical standards for the membership criteria and holds members accountable to honor them.

Practical Tips on Membership

One day only. Don't have a twelve-week membership class. No one is in town that many weeks in a row. Instead, have your membership class in one session. This way, people can schedule it and get all the information you want them to know.

Less is more. Think through what potential members should know and share those things. Trim the fat off your membership class. Most membership classes can be reduced to sixty to ninety minutes. Anything more than that and you might share too much.

What should be taught in a membership class? Teach the history, mission, and vision of your church and the role each member plays. You can also teach your church's core beliefs (although at Calvary we teach this elsewhere). Whatever you decide, you must answer the question, "What must a person know to make an informed decision to join this church?"

Not everyone will join. The sign of a healthy membership system is that not everyone will join. When your vision is clear, some won't be going in that direction and will want to find another church to attend. Your membership class exists to explain to potential members who you are as a church. If you do that well, some people will decide not to join, but most will join because a clear vision is difficult to resist.

Members only. There should be areas of your church in which only members can serve. In our church, only members can be small group leaders. When a person wants to lead a small group, we check if they are a member. If they aren't, we sign them up for our next membership class. This is important because we want people in positions that speak into the lives of others to be aligned with our church's vision and mission.

Removing a member. There will be times when members aren't upholding the membership covenant. There isn't a personal problem keeping them from following through; instead, it is simply rebellion. The action to take is to confront them lovingly and ask why they aren't upholding the membership covenant. When they give their reason, ask them to correct it in a specific period. Then, let them know you will follow up with them after that period has elapsed.

If the members still haven't corrected the situation, contact them again and let them know that, because of their failure to uphold the membership covenant, you are removing them from the membership roll. They are still welcome to attend the church, and should they resolve this problem, they can reapply for membership.

If you want membership to matter, make it matter. A healthy membership process can make a church even healthier by raising the commitment level and giving the entire church alignment in its mission. Membership is as important as you make it, so make it matter.

What are some pitfalls churches fall into when promoting their church?

We've already outlined many pitfalls in this book. One I did not mention, however, is that marketing in general is meant to reach people who need a little push to make the decision to attend your church. Church marketing isn't meant to convince the most hardened of sinners to attend your church next Sunday. I'm not saying this isn't possible; it's simply not the focus.

Here's what I mean: when we do direct mail, one thing we do is remove anyone from other religions from the list because, although

God wants everyone to be saved, our marketing efforts probably aren't the primary way we'll reach them. We must love them and share the gospel with them at the appropriate moment. Usually when someone converts from another faith, apologetics and the answering of difficult questions are involved. Although it is possible, it's unlikely that a person who grew up Muslim will walk away from three generations of tradition because your postcard looked so nice.

Direct mail, Facebook ads, Google AdWords, and placement ads are all geared for those whom God has been working on and who need a little push in your church's direction. This is important because it affects how you will communicate in your copy and when you will promote the church. But you must understand what church promotion can and can't do. It can't change someone's mind about God. However, it can pique people's curiosity and lead them to attend your church for the first time.

You don't become a marketing expert overnight. Take a step. Start doing something. Learn from your mistakes. Celebrate your successes. Pass on what you've learned. In the end, do all you can do to reach your community and see those far from God reconciled to the Father.

Conclusion

Are You Ready to Become a Magnetic Church?

*P*astor Willie planted a church in the inner city of downtown Miami. After five years of ministry, his church had an average attendance of fifty people. He had never tried any promotional outreach to let the community know about his church.

After hearing me speak at a conference, Willie joined Church Ninja. After a few months of learning the strategies outlined in *Pull*, he decided to invest the few dollars he had into his Easter outreach. He called me one day and said, "Pastor Bob, I've never done anything like this before, but I trust that God can use what you've taught me to reach people in my community who so desperately need the gospel."

Willie mobilized his congregation, sent some strategic postcards to his neighborhood, and did some practical ministry the weekend before Easter. When Easter Sunday came, more than 250 people packed his church. It was by far the largest attended service in his church's history.

Andrew planted a church in South Carolina, and after a year of frustration, he joined Church Ninja, hoping to learn some strategies that would help him reach his city. We walked him through the same strategies laid out in *Pull*, and what God has done in his church has been amazing. I'll let Andrew tell you in his words:

> Bob, I've been learning from you for over a year now. It took me about three months to begin to grasp all of the concepts. . . . After that, we've been seeing God do incredible things through quick and steady growth. I want you to know the impact Church Ninja has had on my church and me. I wish more pastors would invest in this program. Over the last nine months, we've baptized more people than the entire history of our church. We've had a few "shots in the arm" by implementing mini-Easters where we instantly doubled and even tripled in size. People have been saved at these events. We've recently used your "Welcome to the Neighborhood" resources to partner with an apartment complex for outreach. (I was shocked the first time a guest came through this ministry, but now I expect this!) This past Sunday, we ran out of chairs for the first time. Our small groups have tripled. Leading a diverse church in a segregated community puzzled our leadership until you explained the term *psychographics*. We've figured out our psychographics and can lead better now. We expect greater things, and it has been fun and challenging to do follow-up and baptisms from these outreach services.

Louis is a young pastor who took over a flailing church of thirty-five people down the street from Calvary. This church struggled for years before Louis's arrival. He joined Church Ninja a few months before his first Easter at the church. I'll let Louis tell you this amazing story in his words.

> Thank you so much for being kingdom-minded and sharing what has worked for you with other church leaders. We implemented what we could in our context. To the glory of our Savior, on Easter Sunday, we had a total of 647 (counting kids) in three services at our church. You know the history of our church and know that for our church, that's HUGE! More than twenty adults and thirty-two kids gave their lives to Christ in our services.

The common denominator is that every one of these leaders learned new skills and put those skills to work to reach his community. I can't promise that God will do in your church what he has done in these churches. However, I do know that God uses activity more than inaction. My encouragement to you is that you put the principles of *Pull* into practice in your church.

I sometimes wonder what the apostle Paul would have done if he had a MacBook Air and an internet connection. I believe he would have used every available means to reach people who didn't know Jesus. He traveled on foot, by horse, by land and sea to preach the gospel. Paul would have done whatever it takes to get the gospel out with the means available today. In that spirit, we should use every means to reach those far from God.

> How, then, can they call on the one they have not believed in? And how can they believe in the one of whom they have not heard? And how can they hear without someone preaching to them? And how can anyone preach unless they are sent? As it is written: "How beautiful are the feet of those who bring good news!" (Rom. 10:14–15 NIV)

Now it's up to you. Are you ready for your church to become magnetic? Are you ready for your church to reach more people than you thought possible? We need your church to step out, take a risk, and do everything in its power to reach those in your city who don't know Jesus. It's our moment to fulfill the Great Commission and take our place in the long line of evangelistic churches that have gone before us.

> I would sooner bring one sinner to Jesus Christ than unravel all the mysteries of the divine Word, for salvation is the one thing we are to live for.
>
> Charles H. Spurgeon

Appendix

The Beginning of *Begin*

I became a Christian just prior to starting college. My older brother shared the gospel with me, and I prayed to receive Christ as my Savior and Lord while sitting at his kitchen table in Boston. I came home to Miami a few days later, excited about my newfound faith but clueless about what steps to take. I attended church and tried to read the Bible, but I felt directionless. My growth as a Christian was slow at best. Thankfully, I eventually attended Bible college, where I was given a clear curriculum that helped me mature. Several years later I was ordained and eventually planted Calvary Fellowship in 2000.

Here's the thing: not everyone has the calling or opportunity to spend years studying the Bible.

As pastors and leaders we are all looking to bridge the gap between new believers and mature believers. The problem we face is there's very little in the way of resources geared toward helping new believers take their first few steps in the faith.

At Calvary, we see hundreds of new believers every month, so I went searching for a book that outlined the basics of the Christian faith in a way that a layperson could understand. New believers often do not understand theological terms, so the book had to explain what young Christians need to know and explain biblical terms along the way.

Eventually, I decided to write *Begin: First Steps for the Journey of Faith*. It's a simple explanation of what it means to be a Christian and how to take your first steps as a follower of Jesus.

At Calvary, we give this book to every person who decides to follow Jesus. We do this for several reasons. First, giving a gift (such as a book) allows us to capture contact information and follow up with each new believer. The reality is, you cannot follow up with people whose contact information you don't have.

Second, *Begin* is a practical tool that is short enough for new believers to read, and the content is intended specifically for them. I have found that if a book is too long, many new believers will not finish it. They grow discouraged and stagger in their new walk with God. *Begin* is long enough to share the most important content new believers need to know and short enough to keep their attention.

Third, *Begin* gives new believers clear direction on what they need to know and do as they start their walk with God. It is a road map that teaches them what it means to be a Christian as well as how to pray, how to read the Bible, and the importance of baptism.

On a recent Sunday I was speaking with a man who had given his life to Jesus during an invitation at the end of one of our services. He had been released from prison on Saturday night and came to church the following morning. It's amazing how God orchestrates seasons of our lives. He spent years paying a high price for a poor choice, and the following morning he made the best decision a person can make. After giving his life to Jesus, he asked the question that most new believers ask: "What's next?" That man, just like every other new believer, needs clear direction and simple steps that will lead from infancy to maturity in Christ. *Begin* is the road map that will get young believers from where they are to where God wants them to be.

A sample of the book follows, as well as some information about how to order more copies at a discount. I hope you find it as useful in your church as we have found it in ours.

Introduction

My Story

My spiritual journey began when I was young. My parents weren't very religious people, but they thought highly of religious education. From third through eighth grade, I attended a parochial school near my house. That's where I learned about God and different aspects of the Bible. I was taught various prayers to say at specific times, and I was educated on who the major players are in the Bible. I even participated in services that probably once had rich meaning but by the time I learned them had become routine and shallow.

I was taught *about* God, but I was never introduced *to* God. God was explained to me the way a teacher gives information about a former world leader or historic figure. I was taught that God is "out there somewhere" but was never told that he is close to me.

My parents are divorced. Each has been married more than once, which makes my family tree look like a two-year-old drew it. I have two sisters and a brother, but my two sisters aren't related. This felt odd to me as I was growing up—odd enough to make God seem distant to what mattered in my life. So I went through adolescence with a pseudo-faith. I believed in God. I even believed that Jesus was God's Son who died on a cross so I could be forgiven, but that never meant anything to me. "Faith" never crossed paths with real life—never, that is, until May 29, 1993.

A New Understanding

I was nineteen and visiting my older brother, who lives in Boston; he had given his life to Christ. Now, this confused me because I thought we were already Christian. I mean, we were Catholic, but I thought that it was all the same thing, the way Coke, Pepsi, and RC are all types of cola, just different flavors.

When I saw my brother and spent some time with him, I realized that our understandings of God were different. It's not that we believed differently; I was amazed at how much we agreed about spiritual things. When my brother spoke about God, he spoke as if he were talking about someone he knew, as if he and God had just gotten off the phone.

My understanding of God was based on facts. I knew about how he created the world in six days, how he once caused it to flood, and how he parted the Red Sea (okay, I got that from the movie *Bruce Almighty*, but it's in the Bible too). My brother talked about a new creation, a re-creation of a human life that yields itself to God. He spoke of a flood of forgiveness God sent in his direction because of what Jesus had done for him. He explained the miracles God performed in his life. For some reason, these things were more spectacular to me than a sea parting down the middle, maybe because they were more tangible.

I awoke the next morning in my brother's house, full of questions. I sat at his kitchen table, and we talked for the next few hours. He didn't just share facts about how Jesus died on the cross, how humans are sinners, and that the Bible is God's book. He told me how all these things matter today. He explained that, as a person, when I do something wrong, I become separated from God because I have failed to meet God's standard. But in his love, God sent Jesus to be the sacrifice that covered all sins I committed. Because of this act of love, through my faith in Jesus, I can spend eternity with God. Meanwhile, I can have a real life here on Earth, in a relationship with God. Through the sacrifice of Jesus, I am no longer separated from God.

I was confused. I told him, "But I already believe in God." Then he explained to me that there's a difference between faith and belief. We believe many things without putting our faith in them. How many smokers believe smoking is unhealthy? Most of them. But that belief doesn't change their habits. How many people believe that being overweight isn't good for them? Most of them. Believing something is true and having the courage to take a step to walk in that truth are different things. That's where faith comes in.

Faith requires acting on the beliefs we have. This is where my brother and I were different. He had faith, and I had only a belief. So he invited me to pray and put my faith in Jesus and become a Christian. This wasn't an invitation into a religious system; I already had that. This was an invitation into a relationship, a connection with God. That's why God asks us to call him Father. It's a word of connection and relationship.

I decided to pray and ask Jesus to forgive me. I asked God to set my life on a new path and to give me peace. What's amazing is that he did! God changed my life. And if you're reading this, either God has done this in your life, or you want him to do it.

Welcome to Miami

A few days after becoming a Christian, I had to go home to Miami, where I lived with my mom and younger sister. I was nineteen and in college, but I didn't know any Christians or what to do with my newfound faith. I started attending a great church, and with the help of people there, I learned some basics of the Christian faith and steps to growing spiritually.

As I look back on my spiritual journey, I see five decisions that helped me tremendously in growing in my relationship with God. If you incorporate these into your life, they will help you immensely in your pursuit of knowing God and growing in your faith.

I Decided to Communicate with God Daily

We communicate with God through prayer. Sometimes we make prayer out to be something that only the professionals can do. They use special words such as *thee* and *thou*; they wear special clothes and place their hands a particular way. You might be surprised to know that Jesus didn't pray like that. He didn't teach his disciples to pray like that.

In a conversation about prayer, Jesus said, "And when you come before God, don't turn that into a theatrical production either. All these people making a regular show out of their prayers, hoping for stardom! Do you think God sits in a box seat? Here's what I want you to do: Find a quiet, secluded place so you won't be tempted to role-play before God. Just be there as simply and honestly as you can manage. The focus will shift from you to God, and you will begin to sense his grace" (Matt. 6:5–6 Message).

Don't worry about the words you use, because God knows your heart. Don't worry about whether you're sitting or standing, because God wants to hear from you.

I have three kids I love dearly. When they want to speak to me, the important thing isn't the position of their hands or the formality of their words; it's the genuineness of their heart. That's true with God as well.

Decide to spend some time daily telling God what's happening in your life and what you are thinking and feeling. It will do more for your journey than you know.

I Decided to Learn about God Daily

I was never a reader before I became a Christian. If you aren't a person who reads much, that's okay. But people who grow in their relationship with God spend some time reading the Bible daily. Why? Because in the Bible, we learn things about God we never knew.

I have a box in my office at home with all the letters my wife wrote me while we were dating and she was away at college. I read and reread those letters because I wanted to know her better. The same is true with God. The stories we read in the Bible tell how God worked in the lives of people throughout history. What's amazing is that as you read those stories you learn that God wants to be faithful to you the same way he was faithful to them.

You don't have to read the entire book in one sitting! Just decide to carve out some time daily to spend with God. Think of it this way—if prayer is speaking to God, then spending time reading the Bible is God's opportunity to speak to you. I've learned that if there's something I'm praying about, often the answer can be found in the section of the Bible I'm reading that day.

I Went to Church Weekly

As I wanted to grow in my faith, I thought the best place to be would be around others who wanted to do the same. When I started to attend church, I sang songs from my heart to God. I opened the Bible, and I was taught how to walk with God through a gifted Bible teacher. I got to know some people who became friends with me and helped me along as I took my first few steps, and I could even use the talents God gave me to help others connect with him.

Getting involved in a church regularly is so important. I know we live in a very busy world, but if we don't make the time to cultivate our relationship with God, no one will do it for us. So we must protect our time and prioritize it. All these years later, I have never regretted that decision to go to church regularly.

I Found Some Friends on the Journey

I had many friends when I became a Christian and started to follow Jesus, but I knew that I also needed friends who would help me along in my spiritual journey. As I went to church and got to know people, friendships naturally formed, and I saw my spiritual life soar because of the people I got to know.

I have learned that getting involved in a small group helps tremendously, because there's nothing greater than going through a difficult time and knowing that you're not alone. It's comforting to know people are praying for me and are ready to help in whatever way possible when I have a problem. It makes life a little easier knowing you have a support system of people who love God and love you.

I Went Public with My Faith through Baptism

Baptism is a public symbol of the inward commitment you've made to follow Jesus. Baptism is a command of Jesus. He asks every one of his followers to be baptized in water. Why? Because in baptism we identify with Jesus's death when we go in the water and then identify with Jesus's resurrection when we emerge from the water (see Rom. 6).

When I was baptized, it was a big deal. It was one of the first times when I read something in the Bible that Jesus asked me to do and I obeyed. Baptism has so much rich meaning and depth, but on a practical level it set a pattern of obedience in my life where I wanted to do God's will.

I recognize these five decisions aren't the answer to all life's questions, but they have been a foundation in my life. They have helped me keep taking steps in God's direction. In the following chapters, I will explain each decision I made and give you some tools for growing in your faith.

One of my favorite movie quotations comes from *The Hurricane*, a film starring Denzel Washington about a boxer wrongfully convicted of murder. In the movie, Lesra Martin's character is in a bookstore and picks up a book by Washington's character. The book moves Martin to help Reuben "The Hurricane" Carter get a fair trial and, ultimately, get out of prison. When he rhetorically asks his friends how a book can move a person to act, his friends respond, "Sometimes you pick the book; sometimes the book picks you."

Not only have you picked this book, but this book has also picked you because it contains the tools for spiritual growth that can serve you for a lifetime.

1

What Does It Mean to Be a Christian?

I received a very kind gift for my fourteenth birthday. A family friend gave me a gold chain that was so cool; it made me look like a member of *Miami Vice*. A gold necklace like that probably cost $500 in 1989 when it was given to me. I wore it to school thinking I was the coolest kid in the world. My classmates *oohed* and *aahed* over my recently acquired gold chain, and I internally vowed that I would never take it off.

That lasted for three days. As I left for school on the third day, I looked at myself in the mirror and noticed something—there was a discoloration on my neck. I thought I was turning into the Incredible Hulk because my neck was turning green. My fashionable gold chain had turned green as well because it wasn't gold. It was a fake! I was angry that I had been given a counterfeit rather than the real thing. I learned that not everything is real just because of its label.

So here's my question for you—what is a Christian? There are enough answers to go around. A 2009 Gallup poll showed that 78 percent of Americans consider themselves Christians.[1] An ABC News poll showed that 75 percent of Americans believe they will go to heaven when they die. Another 14 percent of those surveyed believe in heaven as well; they just aren't sure whether they'll get to go in.[2]

In my experience as a pastor, I have found that people give various reasons why they call themselves Christians:

"I'm a Christian because I'm an American."

"I'm a Christian because my parents believed."

"I was born a Christian and grew up in the church."

"I'm a Christian because I'm not Jewish or Muslim."

My problem with these answers is they don't mention the only reason a person is a Christian. Here's the challenge: You can go to church and not be a Christian. You can read the Bible and not be a Christian. You can eliminate bad habits, pray daily, and try to be a moral person and still not be a Christian. All these habits are good, and Christians should do them, but the actions alone don't make a person a believer.

What then is a Christian? A Christian is a person whom God has forgiven through the finished work of Jesus Christ on the cross. The Bible says:

> Once we, too, were foolish and disobedient. We were misled and became slaves to many lusts and pleasures. Our lives were full of evil and envy, and we hated each other. But—"When God our Savior

revealed his kindness and love, he saved us, not because of the righteous things we had done, but because of his mercy. He washed away our sins, giving us a new birth and new life through the Holy Spirit. He generously poured out the Spirit upon us through Jesus Christ our Savior." (Titus 3:3–6)

We are Christians because of the finished work of Jesus on the cross. We are sinners who have fallen short of God's standard. God came to Earth in the person of Jesus and, being fully God and fully man, he died for us and paid the price for our sins. Through our faith in him, we receive forgiveness of our sins and the gift of eternal life.

In the Bible, a law-enforcement officer once asked the apostle Paul the most important question a person can ask: "What must I do to be saved?" Paul responded, "Believe in the Lord Jesus and you will be saved" (Acts 16:31).

Here's the point: being a Christian isn't about what you do; it's about what Jesus has done. He loves you. He died for you. He forgives you when you open your heart to believe.

So how do you know whether you are a Christian? The Bible says it's a good thing to test ourselves to make sure our faith is real. "Examine yourselves to see if your faith is genuine. Test yourselves. Surely you know that Jesus Christ is among you; if not, you have failed the test of genuine faith" (2 Cor. 13:5).

The apostle John was one of the original twelve disciples who followed Jesus. Toward the end of John's life, he wrote a letter to the church at large, letting them know how they can have eternal life and be confident and secure that they are truly Christians. He wrote at the end of 1 John, "I have written this to you who believe in the name of the Son of God, so that you may know you have eternal life" (5:13). So what things did John write that can assure us we are Christians? We'll learn there are four tests to see whether we are Christians.

Test #1—Confess Jesus as Lord

Whoever confesses that Jesus is the Son of God, God abides in him, and he in God. (1 John 4:15)

The first mark of a true Christian is that he or she confesses that Jesus is Lord, which differs from simply believing in God. The Bible says that even demons believe in God and tremble (James 2:19). Confessing Jesus as Lord means calling on God to save you through the finished work of Jesus on the cross. The apostle Paul put it this way: "If you confess with your mouth the Lord Jesus and believe in your heart that God has raised Him from the dead, you will be saved. For with the heart one believes unto righteousness, and with the mouth confession is made unto salvation" (Rom. 10:9–10).

Being a Christian has nothing to do with being a good person or your good deeds outweighing your bad deeds. All these lines of reasoning are variations of saying, "I'm good enough to save myself." The only problem is we can't save ourselves. We cannot deal with the fact that you and I are fallen, broken, sinful people, which is why the Bible tells us to confess with our mouth that Jesus is Lord and believe in our heart that God raised him from the dead. Understand these are not academic exercises. These two acts signify a paradigm shift in a person's life.

Confess with your mouth that Jesus is Lord, saying, "Jesus, you're in charge. You control my life. I resign that position to you. You're the master, and I'm the servant." Making Jesus Lord of your life is not about title; it's about control. It's about giving him the power to lead, direct, and guide you.

Believing in your heart that God raised Jesus from the dead is a statement declaring that, at the cross, my sins were paid for. When I place my trust in that fact—that Jesus is the only one who can save me—that's when the Bible says, "You are saved." We aren't saved because our parents were Christians or because we gave money to a charity last year. Jesus's death and resurrection are what saves us from a life of futility and misery and an eternity separated from God.

Some people think they're too bad and that God would never accept them. However, there's a promise in the Bible that says otherwise. Romans 10:13 tells us, "Whoever calls on the name of the LORD will be saved." It doesn't matter who you are or what you've done; salvation is about who Jesus is (he's God, and he has the power to forgive) and what Jesus has done (he died for us, rose again, and invites us to experience the life he offers us).

Test #2—Obey the Commands of God

> For this is the love of God, that we keep His commandments. And His commandments are not burdensome. (1 John 5:3)

A revelation happens when we're confronted with the commands of God. First, the commands of God show who God is because they show us God's heart toward us. His commands are given to us out of love and a sincere desire for us to live the best life possible. If you have kids (or if you were ever given rules by your parents), then you know your rules for your kids are based in love. You want your kids to be safe, loving, and functioning members of society, so you create boundaries that ensure they have the chance to grow into the best versions of themselves.

God's commands show God's love for us and his desire to lead us to live in a way that will take us into the abundant life he promised us. Jesus said, "I have come that they may have life, and that they may have it more abundantly" (John 10:10). In short, obeying God's commands leads to the best possible life. In a world where most people simply exist and just "get by" with life, Jesus offers a life with depth, meaning, and purpose in him.

The second discovery we find in obeying the commands of God is the revelation of our faith. Our desire to obey God shows our relationship with him. True Christians won't be perfect in their obedience to God; however, they will seek to obey God. True Christians seek to guide their lives by what God says. This doesn't mean Christians never sin. Unfortunately, we are all sinners, and just because you've become a Christian doesn't mean you'll never sin again. However, true Christians will be miserable when they sin because they will know they are living apart from God's guidance.

The Bible says, "Those who have been born into God's family do not make a practice of sinning, because God's life is in them. So they can't keep on sinning, because they are children of God" (1 John 3:9). True followers of Jesus will feel uncomfortable when they sin because the Holy Spirit is working in their lives.

I became a Christian on May 29, 1993, in my brother's kitchen. He shared the gospel with me, and I responded by inviting Jesus Christ into my life to be Savior and Lord. However, the first thing I did after making the most important decision in my life was go to a baseball game.

I grew up in Boston, and I was there visiting my brother when I decided to follow Jesus. So I went to Fenway Park that evening with my girlfriend Carey (now my wife of sixteen years) and looked forward to enjoying the game.

Here's what you need to know about me: before becoming a Christian, I cussed like a sailor who spent all his free time watching *The Usual Suspects*. My language got especially salty when I watched sporting events.

So during the game, when the umpire made a call I didn't agree with, I stood and said, "Why you—" But somehow I stopped, looked around, and sat down. Carey looked at me, wondering what I would say. I turned to her and said, "I'm a Christian now, and I don't think God wants me to talk like that anymore." I had been a Christian for only three hours, and God was already working in my life.

Does this mean I've never said a word I've regretted since that day? Unfortunately, I have. But whenever it happened, I was unhappy about it, and thankfully God has given me victory in this area of my life. You don't enter a state of perfection when you become a Christian. Instead, you come to an awareness of sin, and the Holy Spirit works in your life to give you victory.

Test #3—Build Friendships with Believers

> Everyone who believes that Jesus is the Christ has become a child of God. And everyone who loves the Father loves his children, too. (1 John 5:1)

It's impossible to grow in your faith alone. Christianity was not designed to be practiced in solitude. The Christian faith works best when we are engaged with others in the journey. Jesus had twelve disciples with him almost everywhere he went. We must follow this model as well.

As a young Christian, I wanted to grow in my faith. I didn't know any other Christians, so I thought the best place to find others of like faith was church. It seemed simple enough, but I had never attended a church in my life. Here's what I found when I started to attend a church: I found people headed in the same direction I was—sincere people more than willing to help me in my new faith journey.

Early in my Christian walk, I met a man named Bill. He wasn't a Bible teacher or theologian. He lived three doors down from me and was a construction worker. He invited me to knock on his door whenever I had questions about the Bible. I kept a notebook of all the questions I had.

Once I had two pages of questions, I would knock on his door, and he would graciously spend hours with me answering every inquiry I had about the Scriptures. Those sessions gave me such confidence in God's Word and helped me build my life on God's truths. Godly men such as Bill and many others who befriended me and mentored me are some reasons I still walk with God.

Here's the bottom line: if you're a Christian, go to church. Get involved. Build some friendships with followers of Christ who inspire you with their faith. We'll cover this topic in-depth in chapter 3, but suffice it to say, this decision is one of the best you can make in your life.

Test #4—Grow in Your Love for Others

He who says he is in the light, and hates his brother, is in darkness until now. He who loves his brother abides in the light, and there is no cause for stumbling in him. But he who hates his brother is in darkness and walks in darkness, and does not know where he is going, because the darkness has blinded his eyes. (1 John 2:9–11)

My five-year-old daughter, Mia, recently memorized the Bible passage on the fruit of the Spirit. It's a section in the Bible that talks about what it looks like when the Holy Spirit begins to work in our lives: "But the fruit of the Spirit is love, joy, peace, longsuffering, kindness, goodness, faithfulness, gentleness, self-control. Against such there is no law" (Gal. 5:22–23).

I told her how important it is to hide God's Word in her heart and that God was pleased with her committing sections of the Bible to memory. Mia was so happy. Twenty minutes later, she got into an argument with her three-year-old brother and punched him. So I took her aside and asked, "Mia, is acting like that showing any of the fruit of the Spirit?" She agreed that her actions weren't loving and apologized to her brother.

This is what it looks like when we say we love God and hate our brother. When God transforms your life, you become a more loving person. God changes your heart and gives you compassion and grace for those you wouldn't have any time for previously.

Do you know why John is so passionate about this topic in particular? It's because John wasn't talking about this in theory. God had transformed his life from an angry, overreacting hothead to a person of grace and love.

There's a scene in the Bible where Jesus comes to a town with his disciples, including John, who was a young man at the time. The townspeople aren't interested in Jesus's message of love and grace, and they ask him to leave. When they don't receive Jesus's message, John and his brother James say, "Do you want us to call down fire from heaven and consume them like Elijah did?" (see Luke 9:54). Essentially they were saying, "Lord, they won't receive the message of love, grace, and forgiveness. Do you want us to kill everyone?" This scene and many other encounters earned John and his brother the nickname *Boanerges*, which means "sons of thunder."

Let's fast-forward a few years. After the death and resurrection of Jesus, the same John who wanted to torch a town instead preached the gospel and saw the grace of God save a town. John's name was changed from "son of thunder" to "the apostle of love." How does this transformation happen? It happens when a person has a real encounter with the living God.

So, are you a Christian? The answer to that question comes down to what you've done with the gospel message that Jesus Christ lived a perfect life, died on a cross, and was buried. Three days later he rose from the dead and offers forgiveness and grace to every person who comes to him.

Have you invited Jesus Christ to come into your life and forgive you of your sins? If not, you can pray this prayer and ask God to forgive you because of what Jesus did. He loves you and wants to do great work in your life. So if you're ready, pray:

Dear God, I open my heart and invite you in. I'm sorry for my sins. I turn from them and turn to you. Thank you for sending Jesus to die for me. I receive Jesus as my Savior and Lord. Thank you for saving me. In Jesus's name. Amen.

If you just prayed that prayer and meant it in faith, Jesus Christ has now taken residence in your heart and life! Your decision to follow Jesus means God has forgiven you. God has started to work in your life right now, and you will spend eternity in heaven.

But this isn't the finish line—it's just the starting point. This is the first step to building your life on God's truth. So now that you're a Christian, how do you communicate with God? What do you say? How do you know that God hears you? How do you know whether you're praying the right way? We'll pick up that topic next.

2

Learning to Pray

I remember the first time I prayed out loud in public. I had been a Christian for about four months, and I was in the Atlantic Ocean waiting to be baptized. The church leaders baptizing me asked whether I would pray before professing my faith in Jesus through water baptism.

I was scared to death, but twenty years later, I still remember the terrified prayer I prayed. "God, thanks for everything. I'm here to be baptized. I'm here . . . I'm here, Lord . . . Amen!" Here's what's odd: I had never been nervous praying. I prayed to God throughout the day as someone would talk to a friend. However, when I got around two men whom I considered "spiritual," I froze and couldn't pray. I thought I needed to pepper my prayer with a "thee" and a "thou" to sound holy. I became very self-conscious over every word, and in the end I didn't say much.

This desire we have to impress others (or even impress God) with our prayers is the start of the problem. When we try to impress or sound holy, we miss the point of prayer, which is simply connecting with God. Some people think that the length of your prayers is what makes your time with God special. Here's what I've noted: every recorded prayer of Jesus can be recited in less than two minutes. So if it's not the vernacular of the prayer or the duration of the prayer, what is the key to effective prayer?

Jesus's disciples came to him one day and asked him an important question. They wanted to learn to pray.

> Now it came to pass, as He was praying in a certain place, when He ceased, that one of His disciples said to Him, "Lord, teach us to pray, as John also taught his disciples." (Luke 11:1)

These disciples didn't ask Jesus to teach them to do miracles, to preach, or to walk on water. Instead, they asked him to instruct them in how to connect with the Father in prayer the same way he did. This question didn't surprise Jesus. In ancient Jewish culture, a disciple wanted to learn to do everything like his rabbi, his teacher. True to form, these first-century disciples were seeking to learn the best way to connect with God, which would be the way their rabbi prayed.

Jesus's response to their inquiry is the fifty-nine words we call the Lord's Prayer. It should more adequately be called the Disciples' Prayer because Jesus taught them to pray this prayer. I don't believe Jesus is teaching them that this is the only prayer they should pray. Instead, I believe this prayer is a template for us on how to connect with God in prayer.

Now it came to pass, as He was praying in a certain place, when He ceased, that one of His disciples said to Him, "Lord, teach us to pray, as John also taught his disciples." So He said to them, "When you pray, say:

Our Father in heaven, hallowed be Your name. Your kingdom come. Your will be done on earth as it is in heaven. Give us day by day our daily bread. And forgive us our sins, for we also forgive everyone who is indebted to us.

And do not lead us into temptation, but deliver us from the evil one." (Luke 11:1–4)

Jesus dispelled the myth that answered prayers have to do with the words you use and the length of your prayer. Jesus's prayer is short but potent. I love that what Jesus taught his disciples was countercultural in that day. Rabbis in the first century usually taught the opposite. One famous rabbi wrote, "Whoever is long in prayer is heard." Another said, "Whenever the righteous make their prayer long, their prayer is heard."[3] Jesus focuses on the relationship and the content of the prayer rather than the duration. Yet in this model prayer, Jesus shows us five keys to effective prayer that we can apply to our prayers and know that we pray in the way Jesus taught us.

Our Holy Father

The Jews addressed God by calling him Lord out of reverence. Their respect of God was so extreme that they wouldn't even utter God's name. Yet, when Jesus died for us, he brought us back into relationship with God, and this prayer shows us the relationship we have with him is a Father-child relationship. Why did Jesus instruct us to address God as "our Father"? Because God is not some distant being who's unapproachable and disengaged from our lives. So when we pray, we're reminded that God loves us as a father loves his kids.

When Jesus adds the second phrase of his introduction to this model prayer, he says, "Hallowed be Your name." The word *hallowed* simply means "holy." It shows us that God is separate from humankind. He is good and perfect in all his ways. Jesus wants us to remember this truth because God has our best interests at heart. Even when God doesn't answer our prayers exactly the way we ask, we can be confident that our heavenly Father loves us and always works toward what is in our best interest.

God's Kingdom and God's Will

When I started college, my dad decided to buy me a car. He told me to check out some used cars and find one I really liked. He said the next day he would come with me and we'd buy it. So I went to a few places and browsed the inventory. That's when I saw the perfect vehicle for me. It was a purple lowrider pickup truck. I loved it. It had more than one hundred thousand miles on it, but that didn't matter. All I could picture was my driving it down the road, blasting some music out of it because in the back it had state-of-the-art speakers . . . roughly the size of a coffin.

I took my dad to see it the next day, and he had a much different perspective than I did. He showed me the giant crack in the windshield, the dents all over the truck, and that one door didn't open. I didn't buy the truck. Once I saw things from his perspective, it changed my desire.

The same thing is true with prayer. When Jesus prays, "Your kingdom come. Your will be done on earth as it is in heaven," it's a powerful statement. In heaven, everything happens exactly the way God wants it to. This is God's desire for the earth as a whole and for our lives specifically. This should be our ambition as well. We should seek to live so that God's will is evident in our lives.

> For I know the thoughts that I think toward you, says the LORD, thoughts of peace and not of evil, to give you a future and a hope. (Jer. 29:11)

God's will is to give you a future and a hope. His desire is to give you a life filled with purpose, meaning, and significance. That doesn't mean life will be easy, but it does mean it will be worth it. I want you to notice something: Jesus doesn't teach us to stack our laundry list of requests up front. Instead, he instructs us to realize to whom we're praying—the God of the universe who loves us and wants us to call him Father. Then, once we've acknowledged his holiness, we can bring God our requests.

Daily Bread

Baking bread in the ancient Middle East was a daily activity. Bread was a staple item, and you baked it every day to feed your family. When Jesus teaches us to ask, "Give us this day our daily bread," it's a petition for God's provision in our lives. To this day, I am still blown away that the God of the universe cares about my needs and desires.

> When I look at the night sky and see the work of your
> fingers—
> the moon and the stars you set in place—

what are mere mortals that you should think about them,
human beings that you should care for them? (Ps. 8:3–4)

Another important point to note is that "Give us this day our daily bread" is a reminder that everything we have comes from God. He is our ultimate provider. He gives us the air we breathe, the skills to function in our career, and the resources to purchase life's necessities. It's freeing to realize that I am not the source of everything I need. My loving heavenly Father is the source of everything, and he is willing to provide for me. We can come to him with any request, knowing that he will always answer. He might not answer in the exact way we hope, but he will answer and meet our needs.

Whatever is good and perfect comes down to us from God our Father, who created all the lights in the heavens. (James 1:17)

On Forgiving and Being Forgiven

John, a pastor on my staff, recently loaned his car to a member of our church. However, the member dented his car while driving it back to our office. I heard about the incident, and I asked John what he would do about this.

John said, "I forgave him and told him not to worry about it." I was angry. I told John that this person was irresponsible and that the only way he would learn was if he had to pay for his infraction. John smiled and said, "Bob, the problem is that I borrowed my friend's truck a few weeks ago and I dented it while I was using it, and he forgave me."

I felt a bit foolish. However, I was also reminded of an important lesson on the power of forgiveness. Jesus taught us in the model prayer to say, "And forgive us our sins, for we also forgive everyone who is indebted to us" (Luke 11:4). We can come to God because of forgiveness. When we place our faith in Jesus, we receive his forgiveness for all our sins and trespasses, meaning we have no right to withhold forgiveness from others. Regardless of what someone has done to us, we owed a greater debt to God that was forgiven through Jesus. Forgiveness is difficult because it's not the natural response when we're hurt. Our natural response is revenge because we want the person who hurt us to feel the same pain we feel.

In the Gospels, there's a story in which Jesus has dinner with a religious leader, and as they eat, a woman comes in and pours oil on Jesus's feet. She weeps on his feet and dries the tears with her hair. It's a powerful picture because this woman was a prostitute; in that culture, she was a sinner of the worst kind.

The religious leader thought, "If Jesus were a prophet, he wouldn't even allow this woman to touch him." Jesus then told the man a story that shows his heart and demonstrates to us the true meaning of forgiveness.

"A man loaned money to two people—500 pieces of silver to one and 50 pieces to the other. But neither of them could repay him, so he kindly forgave them both, canceling their debts. Who do you suppose loved him more after that?"

Simon answered, "I suppose the one for whom he canceled the larger debt."

"That's right," Jesus said. Then he turned to the woman and said to Simon, "Look at this woman kneeling here. When I entered your home, you didn't offer me water to wash the dust from my feet, but she has washed them with her tears and wiped them with her hair. You didn't greet me with a kiss, but from the time I first came in, she has not stopped kissing my feet. You neglected the courtesy of olive oil to anoint my head, but she has anointed my feet with rare perfume.

"I tell you, her sins—and they are many—have been forgiven, so she has shown me much love. But a person who is forgiven little shows only little love." (Luke 7:41–47)

If you're a Christian, then you're like that woman. We have been forgiven so much, and therefore we must model forgiveness to others. This is why we pray and thank God for forgiving us, because it makes forgiving others easier.

There's also another reason we need to forgive—because it's the best way to live. When I choose not to forgive, I am trapped in a prison of anger and bitterness. The only way to be released from this prison is to forgive. It's the key to opening the cell and living in freedom.

We don't forgive because we believe we're letting that person who hurt us off the hook. Forgiveness is the way for us to keep the past from controlling us. We all know people who have been hurt by an experience or relationship, and to this day that pain controls their lives because of their refusal to forgive. Forgiveness is the medicine that keeps us from becoming bitter people.

Get rid of all bitterness, rage and anger, brawling and slander, along with every form of malice. Be kind and compassionate to one another, forgiving each other, just as in Christ God forgave you. (Eph. 4:31–32 NIV)

Dealing with Temptation

Jesus closes his model prayer by teaching us to recognize our propensity for sin. We are by nature fallen people, and we need God's power in our lives to avoid the temptation that will hurt us. We should note that when Jesus teaches us to pray, "And do not lead us into temptation, but deliver us from the evil one" (Luke 11:4), he is not saying that God marches us into temptation and then drops us off. Instead, this prayer, as one New Testament paraphrase states, "Keep[s] us clear of temptation."[4]

> Let no one say when he is tempted, "I am tempted by God"; for God cannot be tempted by evil, nor does He Himself tempt anyone. But each one is tempted when he is drawn away by his own desires and enticed. Then, when desire has conceived, it gives birth to sin; and sin, when it is full-grown, brings forth death. (James 1:13–15)

Jesus teaches us to ask God to lead us in a way that we won't be sidetracked and caught by temptation.

We should understand that temptation by itself is not sin. We read in the Gospels that even Jesus was tempted. He never gave in to it, but he was tempted. When you and I are tempted, it's our opportunity to draw close to God, ask for his help and strength, and resist temptation.

> The temptations in your life are no different from what others experience. And God is faithful. He will not allow the temptation to be more than you can stand. When you are tempted, he will show you a way out so that you can endure. (1 Cor. 10:13)

Asking for God's help in temptation is an honest admission of our vulnerabilities. None of us is resistant to temptation. We all struggle. The more honest we are with God, the more open we are to following his lead as we navigate temptation.

The beauty of prayer is that you don't need a theology degree to pray correctly. You can simply talk to God and converse with him throughout your day. You don't have to kneel or light a candle to talk to God. The Bible says, "Pray without ceasing" (1 Thess. 5:17). This doesn't mean you must quit your job and pray twenty-four hours a day. It simply means your life has an attitude of prayer. The words don't have to be eloquent. God simply wants to hear from you.

Notes

1. Frank Newport, "This Christmas, 78% of Americans Identify as Christian," Gallup, December 24, 2009, http://www.gallup.com/poll/124793/this-christmas-78-americans-identify-christian.aspx.

2. Dalia Sussman, "Poll: Elbow Room No Problem in Heaven," ABC News, December 20, 2005, http://abcnews.go.com/US/Beliefs/story?id=1422658.

3. William Barclay, *The Gospel of Matthew* (Louisville: Westminster John Knox, 1975), 225.

4. J. B. Philips, *The New Testament in Modern English* (New York: Touchstone Books, 1958), 140.

Notes

1. Larry Winget, *Shut Up, Stop Whining, and Get a Life: A Kick Butt Approach to a Better Life* (Hoboken, NJ: Wiley & Sons, 2011), 107.

2. Ibid.

3. Jim Collins, *Good to Great* (New York: HarperBusiness, 2001), 13.

4. Sam Chand, *Cracking Your Church's Culture Code: Seven Keys to Unleashing Vision and Inspiration* (San Francisco: Jossey-Bass, 2010), 4.

5. C. H. Spurgeon, *The Soulwinner* (New Kensington, PA: Whitaker House, 1995), 212.

6. Dennis Gaffney, "Essay: What Made DiMaggio a Great Player?" special features, *Joe DiMaggio: The Hero's Life*, PBS American Experience, 2000, http://www.pbs.org/wgbh/amex/dimaggio/sfeature/essay.html.

7. Dan and Chip Heath, *Made to Stick: Why Some Ideas Survive and Others Die* (New York: Random House, 2007), 20–21.

8. Dan Kennedy, *The Ultimate Marketing Plan* (Avon, MA: Adams Media, 1991), 23.

9. KISSmetrics blog, "Facebook Statistics," http://blog.kissmetrics.com/facebook-statistics/.

10. Sharon Gaudin, "Facebook Passes Google as Most Visited Site of 2010," *Computerworld,* January 2, 2011, http://www.computerworld.com/s/article/9202938/Facebook_passes_Google_as_most_visited_site_of_2010.

11. KISSmetrics blog, "Facebook Statistics."

12. Caitlin A. Johnson, "Cutting through Advertising Clutter," CBS News, February 11, 2009, http://www.cbsnews.com/8301-3445_162-2015684.html.

13. "Direct Mail Guru: Did You Know?" Select Mailing, 2012, http://selectmailing.com/guru_whystillworks.html.

Bob Franquiz is the founding and senior pastor of Calvary Fellowship in Miami, FL (www.calvarywired.com). Bob is also the founder of Church Ninja (www.churchninja.com), an organization that provides training and resources to pastors and church leaders. Bob's other books include *Elements: Starting a Revolution in Your World* and *Zero to Sixty: 60 Principles and Practices for Leading a Growing Church.* Prior to entering pastoral ministry, Bob played guitar for Christian hardcore band Strongarm, a band that has been called one of the best Christian metal bands of all time. Before planting Calvary Fellowship, Bob served as an assistant pastor at Calvary Chapel Fort Lauderdale, one of the ten largest churches in America. His primary role was as dean of Calvary Chapel Bible College, where he trained future pastors, ministry leaders, and church planters. Bob considers his greatest achievement being married to Carey, his "just out of high school" sweetheart, for the last sixteen years. Together, they have three beautiful children: Mia, Alexander, and Olivia.

If you're tired of throwing away thousands of dollars on outreach and want to see your church grow as much as 35% this year, **then test drive Church Ninja for just $1.**

Church Ninja Focuses on the Seven Secrets to Effective Outreach:

1. Evangelistic Culture
2. Targeted Market
3. Trackable Results
4. Eye-Catching Design
5. Effective Follow-Up
6. Healthy Team
7. Strategic Budgeting

Visit churchninja.com/pull and take the TEST DRIVE for just $1.

Follow Bob Franquiz:
Twitter: @bobfranquiz
Facebook: fb.com/bobfranquiz
Instagram: bobfranquiz

www.churchninja.com

Leadership Ninja is a step by step program that gives you all the tools you need to develop leaders at every level and see them grow to maturity.

What's Covered in Leadership Ninja?

1. Leadership Development from the Ground Up
2. The Art of Strategic Investment
3. Turning Your Audience into an Army
4. Leading Yourself
5. Building Your Dream Team
6. Coaching a Championship Caliber Team
7. The Science of Casting Vision
8. Evaluating Your Team
9. Laying a Solid Foundation
10. Dollars and Sense

Follow Bob Franquiz:
Twitter: @bobfranquiz
Facebook: fb.com/bobfranquiz
Instagram: bobfranquiz

www.ninjaleadership.com

For the New Believers
IN YOUR MINISTRY

When someone becomes a new Christian, they are often left wondering what to do next. What does it mean to be a Christian? Where do they start?

Begin provides a road map for new Christians. New Christians will discover the practices that encourage spiritual growth and develop a process that allows them to keep growing closer to God for a lifetime.